HISTORIC TALES *of* WILBRAHAM

HISTORIC TALES *of* WILBRAHAM

DAVID F. BOURCIER

THE History PRESS

Published by The History Press
An imprint of Arcadia Publishing
Charleston, SC
www.historypress.com

First published 2025

Manufactured in the United States

ISBN 9781467159425

Library of Congress Control Number: 2025931960

CONTENTS

ACKNOWLEDGMENTS

My lifelong love affair with local history has been a source of immense joy, particularly as I navigated the charming landscape of Wilbraham during my formative years. The neighborhood's steadfast embrace of nineteenth-century charm infused my childhood with a unique and captivating atmosphere, sparking an early curiosity about the rich mosaic of stories embedded in the very essence of my surroundings at 6 Chapel Street, Wilbraham.

Amid this historical haven, two figures stand out as catalysts for my deeper exploration into the past: my next-door neighbors Andy and Barbara Nygren. Their shared passion for history served as a beacon, guiding my journey into the layers of time that enveloped Wilbraham.

The Nygrens' residence at 3 Chapel Street emerged as a living testament to bygone eras. Constructed in 1879 by Barbara's grandparents Erasmus B. and Harriet Gates, the house became an embodiment of the town's history. Erasmus—a man of multifaceted roles as a store owner, cofounder of a textile mill on Twelve Mile Brook, postmaster and town official—played a pivotal role in shaping Wilbraham's narrative.

The torch of community engagement passed seamlessly through generations, landing in the capable hands of Barbara's parents Myra Gates and Walter F. Berry. Their contributions to local government, businesses and various civic duties underscored a commitment to not just live in Wilbraham but to actively participate in its evolution.

Above: Chapel Street in the early 1900s. *Wilbraham Public Library.*

Opposite: The family: David, Kelley, Lindsey and Marty. *David F. Bourcier.*

The Nygren home, more than a physical structure, evolved into a living museum curated by a family deeply connected to the town's past. Andy and Barbara Nygren, as avid historians themselves, generously shared the stories embedded within those walls, offering me a front-row seat to the fascinating history of Wilbraham.

For a history enthusiast like myself, the Nygrens' narrative goes beyond the pages of a textbook; it is a living, breathing account of a town's evolution. Their passion has not only enriched my understanding of Wilbraham's past but has also inspired me to continue uncovering the hidden gems that contribute to the unique richness of local history. In the footsteps of the Nygrens, I explore, learn and cherish the timeless stories that define my beloved hometown.

Since my retirement in 2019 from the position of Wilbraham's fire chief, I've rekindled my passion for local history. I owe a tremendous debt of gratitude to my wife, Kelley, and our daughter, Lindsey, for their unwavering support in my renewed research endeavors. Lindsey, who shares my fascination with history, played a pivotal role in providing me with the tools and assistance to launch the Wilbraham Historical Tidbits website in 2021. She is also a valued contributing editor on the site.

A few years into this historical journey, spurred by my daughter's encouragement, I found myself contemplating the idea of writing this book.

This envisioned compilation would consist of short stories inspired by the true historical events of Wilbraham and the surrounding area. The success of this venture is undoubtedly owed to the steadfast support of my family, particularly Kelley and Lindsey, who have been my pillars throughout. Special mention must also be made of Marty, our loyal Shih Tzu dog, who has faithfully kept me company by my side during the countless hours spent on this enriching project.

INTRODUCTION

Wilbraham, Massachusetts, is steeped in a captivating history that traces its roots back to the vibrant presence of Native Americans. Among the earliest inhabitants were the Agawam, Nipmuc and Wampanoag tribes, each contributing to the shaping of the land now known as Wilbraham. The Nipmuc Indians, in particular, left an indelible mark by utilizing the area as a versatile three-season camping ground.

Their strategic use of the Connecticut River, Chicopee River and Twelve Mile Brook showcased a sophisticated understanding of the natural resources available. The Nipmuc Indians engaged in a diverse range of activities, including trapping beaver in streams, spearing salmon in river waters, hunting deer and fowl and gathering an array of berries and nuts. The fertile agricultural land in the northwest and southeast, coupled with the abundance of fish in the Chicopee River, provided essential sustenance.

Key geographical features like Spectacle and Nine Mile Ponds added to the richness of the landscape, offering prime locations for interior stream fishing. The wooded uplands and marshlands likely served as vital sites for hunting and gathering, contributing to the self-sufficiency of these Indigenous communities.

Historical evidence suggests that during the Plantation Period (1620–75), the Native American inhabitants primarily occupied sections along Nine Mile Pond, the Chicopee River, Spectacle Pond (Spec Pond) and the hilly mountain area. This period marked a time of coexistence and utilization of the land's resources, as these communities thrived in harmony with their surroundings.

The steatite (soapstone) quarry at the northern end of Glendale Road played a vital role in the lives of these early inhabitants for thousands of years. This quarry, a source of soapstone, yielded various implements that enhanced their lives through trade and as durable tools. Items such as bowls, pipes, arrowheads, hammers, plow heads and mortar and pestles were crafted from soapstone, evidencing a sophisticated use of resources.

The Native American artifacts, including those from the soapstone quarry, provide a glimpse into the ingenuity and craftsmanship of the Indigenous people. Many of these artifacts are on display at the Quadrangle Museums in Springfield, and the Old Meeting House Museum in Wilbraham preserves a significant collection as well.

Noteworthy is the Wigwam Hill, named after an old "Indian" woman named Weshaugan, who continued to live in Wilbraham after the broader Native American community likely abandoned the area after King Philip's War in 1675. Her presence adds a personal touch to the historical landscape.

A similar soapstone quarry existed in Westfield, Massachusetts, emphasizing the importance of these quarries in the Pioneer Valley. The impact of this soapstone extraction echoes beyond Wilbraham, contributing to the wider archaeological and historical narrative of the region.

The Springfield Science Museum further commemorates this history with a Native American exhibit, showcasing a soapstone boulder from the Wilbraham quarry. Removed in 1933, this boulder features a partly finished bowl in relief, providing a tangible link to the craftsmanship of the past. Wilbraham's history, deeply rooted in the narratives of its Native American inhabitants, serves as a testament to the resilience and resourcefulness of these communities.

In 1674, a noteworthy land transaction took place in the region now known as Wilbraham Ludlow and Hampden, Massachusetts. William Pynchon of Springfield acquired a significant tract of land stretching to Springfield Mountain from the Nipmuc Indians. The sellers were three individuals named Wequagan, Wawapaw and Wequampo. The unique aspect of this transaction lay in its simplicity, involving only three Native Americans who sold the land for a fathom of wampum, equivalent to six feet of strung shell beads.

The term *wampum* finds its origin in the Narragansett language, referring to "white shell beads" sourced from the whelk shell. Notably, a white wampum fathom held considerable value, amounting to ten shillings or half a pound or half a sovereign in currency.

Despite the completion of the transaction, the Nipmuc individuals faced displacement due to the outbreak of the Indian War in 1675. This unfortunate turn of events interrupted their connection to the land they had sold just a year earlier. The details of the land purchase were officially recorded for the County of Hampshire on July 12, 1679, with John Holyoke serving as the attesting recorder. This historical record can be explored in the Registry of Deeds in Hampden County.

Importantly, the agreement between Pynchon and the Nipmuc Indians included a provision that allowed the Native Americans to retain their rights for hunting and fishing on the land. This acknowledgment reflected a recognition of their long-standing connection to the territory.

Over time, the area known as Minnechaug or Berryland, as acquired by Pynchon, eventually evolved into the town of Wilbraham. The town received its official incorporation in 1763, solidifying its place in history as a settlement with a unique origin rooted in Native American land transactions and the subsequent development of colonial New England.

The pre-incorporation history of Wilbraham unfolds with the arrival of Nathaniel Hitchcock in the summer of 1730. Departing from the settled community of Springfield along the Connecticut River, Hitchcock ventured to the Outward Commons, also named Springfield Mountain. There he diligently cleared and cultivated two acres of land, constructing a log hut on the west side of what is now known as 603 Main Street, Wilbraham. After sowing his two acres of wheat, Hitchcock returned to Springfield for the winter.

In May 1731, Hitchcock made a triumphant return with his wife, Hannah Taylor, whom he had married the previous year, and their four-month-old daughter, also named Hannah. The family committed to making this wilderness their year-round residence, facing the challenges of isolation in an untamed landscape. Over the subsequent years, they expanded their family with four more children: Nathaniel, Mary, Gideon and Silas. Notably, their closest neighbors were a distant nine miles away in the Springfield settlement along the Connecticut River.

During his first year, Hitchcock engaged in various agricultural activities, from planting corn and gathering wheat to mowing grass, drying and stacking hay and husking and storing corn. The winter months provided solace with the music of his wife's songs and the playful voices of their children.

As the following spring arrived, marked by the return of robins and bluebirds, Wilbraham began to witness the gradual settlement of more families. Notably, Noah Alvord and his wife, Hannah Burt, accompanied

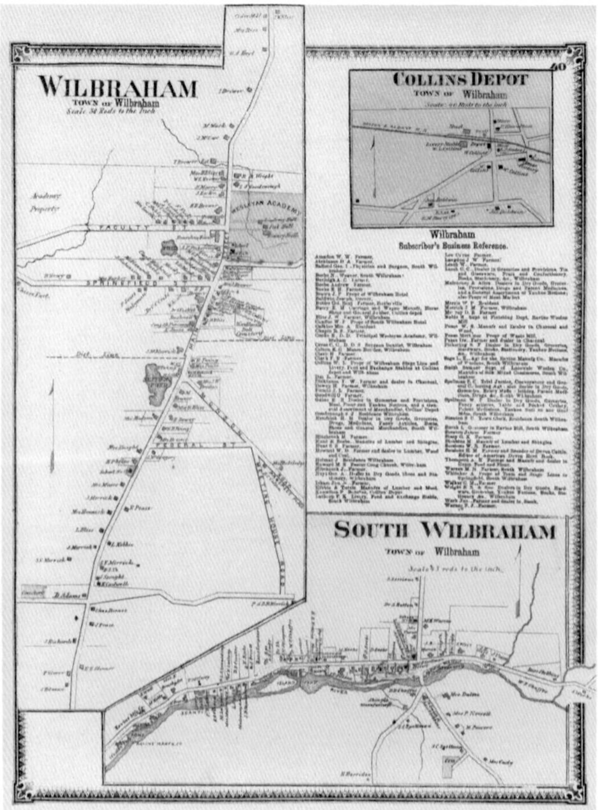

An 1870 map of Wilbraham. *Atlas of Hampden County.*

by their two children, Hannah and Moses, established their homestead just six hundred feet south of the Hitchcock residence on the east side of West Road, now 648 Main Street, Wilbraham. The Alvord family expanded with the addition of two more children, Aaron and Elizabeth, although none of them produced a next generation.

This initial settlement marked the beginning of Wilbraham's community development, as more families were drawn to the promise of a good and sustainable life in this picturesque and fertile area. The collective efforts of these early settlers laid the groundwork for the future town of Wilbraham, shaping its character and contributing to its enduring history.

Exploring the historical accounts of Wilbraham reveals a collection of exciting stories based on true events. These narratives not only provide a captivating glimpse into the past but also offer a profound understanding of how our town evolved into the vibrant community we know today. Each tale is a thread in the rich fabric of our history, weaving together the struggles, triumphs and everyday lives of the people who laid the foundation for our town.

As we delve into these pages, we embark on a journey that brings history alive, allowing us to connect with the experiences of those who shaped Wilbraham. From the earliest settlers carving a life out of the wilderness to the gradual growth of the community, these stories unfold with a sense of adventure and resilience. The challenges faced, the bonds forged and the landmarks established all contribute to the unique identity of our town.

By immersing ourselves in these narratives, we gain a deeper appreciation for the roots that anchored Wilbraham in the past. The characters come to life, their endeavors echoing through time, reminding us of the shared heritage that unites us. This exploration of our history is not just a collection of facts but a celebration of the spirit that has propelled Wilbraham forward.

As we turn the pages, let the excitement of rediscovering our town's history inspire us to cherish and preserve the legacy handed down by those who came before. May these stories serve as a reminder of the strength and resilience embedded in our community, contributing to the ongoing narrative of Wilbraham.

ABIGAIL AND THE PARSON'S ROSE OF 1744

On a fateful day in history, May 26, 1741, the esteemed Mr. Noah Mirick (nowadays spelled "Merrick") accepted his nomination as the inaugural minister of the Fourth Precinct of Springfield, a picturesque locale known as "Springfield Mountain" in the expansive Outward Commons. Born in West Springfield on August 6, 1711, he was the beloved son of James and Sarah (Hitchcock) Mirick.

Noah Mirick's journey to this esteemed position was a tale woven with the threads of education and friendship. While attending Yale College in the charming town of New Haven, Connecticut, he found lodging in the residence of Reverend Phineas Fiske of Haddam. It was there that he crossed paths with Fiske's daughter, Abigail, born on August 14, 1718. Over time, a deep friendship blossomed between Noah and Abigail.

In 1731, Noah Mirick, alongside his close friend Chiliab Brainerd, graduated from Yale College, their minds enriched with knowledge. Noah continued to delve into theology under the guidance of Reverend Phineas Fiske, one of the early tutors and founders of Yale College. Reverend Fiske's influence extended to the college's location, as he played a pivotal role in establishing it in New Haven instead of Saybrook.

The official inauguration of Reverend Noah Merrick took place on June 24, 1741, the same day the church was formed. The ordination council was initially planned to convene under the shade of a mighty oak tree within Daniel Warner's property on West Road (576 Main Street, Wilbraham). However, a twist of fate unfolded as ominous clouds gathered overhead. Just as the service commenced, the heavens opened up, and the congregation hastily relocated to Nathaniel Warriner's barn just south of this place (599 Main Street), where the sacred ordination ceremony unfolded.

During his college years, Noah had forged enduring friendships, notably with Abigail Fiske and Reverend Chiliab Brainerd. In 1736, Abigail and Chiliab joined their lives in marriage, embarking on a shared journey in faith. Tragically, in 1739, Chiliab passed away in Glastonbury, Connecticut, at the tender age of thirty-one, leaving behind a grieving widow and community.

A significant moment in the history of this community occurred on May 4, 1742, when the decision was made to construct Reverend Noah Merrick's residence on Wigwam Hill, a portion of the over-plus land in the middle division, located in the area of 1347 Tinkham Road. The exact location of the Meeting House at 1339 Tinkham Road, a central hub for

Noah Merrick's personal account book. *Merrick family.*

the community, was the subject of extensive debate. However, after much discussion, the decision was finalized on March 15, 1748. Construction was completed, and the meeting house was first used later that same year. This site was nestled southwest of Reverend Noah Merrick's home. Before this development, Nathaniel Hitchcock's residence at 603 Main Street served as a temporary venue for precinct meetings and public worship.

In October 1744, a significant event marked a turning point in Reverend Noah Merrick's life, as he married Abigail (Fisk) Brainerd, the widow of his dear friend from Haddam, Connecticut. Their shared journey is documented in Reverend Merrick's personal account book, which details numerous trips to Haddam between 1741 and 1744. Notably, during one of their horseback journeys to his parish, Abigail brought with her some rose bush slips from her ancestral home, planting them near their new dwelling on Wigwam Hill. She generously shared these slips with neighbors, family and friends, resulting in a proliferation of these roses throughout the Outward Commons. These roses, descendants of the original Parson's Rose, can still be found today in various parts of the town, a testament to Abigail's enduring legacy. Extensive research has revealed that this particular rose is a Damask Rose, renowned for its fragrance and significance in the world of horticulture.

Together, Abigail and Noah raised a family of seven children, further solidifying their bond. In addition to their own children, they welcomed Abigail's daughter from her previous marriage, making a total of eight cherished children:

- Noah Merrick (1745–1762). Tragically, Noah met an untimely end at the age of sixteen in Cambridge, Massachusetts Colony, British Colonial America, succumbing to drowning while pursuing an education at Harvard College.
- Sarah Merrick (1747–1814)
- Chileab Brainerd Merrick (1749–1833)
- Samuel Fisk Merrick (1751–1836)
- Lydia Merrick (1753–1834)
- Pliny Merrick (1755–1814)
- Lucy Merrick (1757–1757)

The legacy of Reverend Noah Merrick is a vital chapter in the annals of this community. He served as the spiritual leader for thirty-six years, dedicating his life to the well-being of his parishioners. His earthly journey came to an end on December 22, 1776, but his memory and impact endure.

On Christmas Day, he was laid to rest at the Burying Yard (Adam's Cemetery). Abigail, his faithful companion, continued her earthly journey until the age of eighty-nine, passing away on September 12, 1807. She lies beside her beloved husband Noah, their love story etched in the history of Wilbraham.

Noah Merrick's shoe buckle. *Atheneum Society of Wilbraham.*

The tale of the Parson's Rose, cherished and passed down through generations, adds a touch of enchantment to this narrative. Chauncy E. Peck, in his historical account of Wilbraham in 1913, recounted this story, which was originally shared with him by his great-aunt, a close neighbor of Mrs. Merrick in her youth. This story resurfaced in 1904 when a town resident gifted Peck's family with a bouquet of roses, labeling them the Parson's Rose. Touched by this connection to history, Chauncy composed a poem titled "The Parson's Rose," a beautiful testament to the enduring legacy of Abigail's rose bushes and the love story that inspired them.

The Parson's Rose represents not only a fragrant symbol of the past but also a reminder of the enduring impact of deeds and love, which, like the roses, continue to bloom in the hearts and minds of those who remember the story. This tale of love, friendship and the fragrant Parson's Rose continues to captivate the imagination, a true Wilbraham story that bridges generations and eras.

THE MELANCHOLY MURMURS OF NABBY'S TEA LEAVES

In the quiet town of Wilbraham, nestled beneath rolling hills, the year was 1799, and spring was breathing life into the land. Gordon Bliss, a promising young man with a legal mind, graduated from Dartmouth College in 1797, and after completing two years of study, he was admitted to the Massachusetts Bar. In celebration of his accomplishments, his mother, Martha, and his father, Levi, beamed with pride, determined to make his brief stay a time of joy and respite.

The Bliss household buzzed with energy as Gordon regaled the eager audience with tales of his adventures in Hanover and Boston. The young people of the town gathered around the hearth, captivated by his stories of college escapades and the allure of the outside world. The elders, intrigued by tales of city life, questioned Gordon eagerly, especially about bustling Boston.

On a fair April day, the sun kissed the earth, inviting laughter and camaraderie. The Bliss home played host to a final gathering before Gordon embarked on his legal career in the city. Young men and women basked in the warmth of April, cherishing each moment before their paths diverged.

As the young men exchanged stories and laughter, the young ladies convened in the front room for a formal tea. Amid the cups and saucers, Abigail "Nabby" Merrick playfully decided to read her fortune from tea leaves, a custom of the time. She turned her cup over, eyes widening as she exclaimed, "Oh, I'm going to be drowned!" The others chuckled, brushing off the ominous words.

The idea of a pleasure boat ride surfaced, perhaps as an effort to cast aside the dark prediction. At the heart of the plan, was it a pursuit of adventure, a challenge or perhaps a way to defy the foretold fate? Nabby's jests might have ignited the spark, a call to fate to prove her wrong. However, the truth lay shrouded in the mists of history.

Soon after, the proposition was made and agreed to by some of the company to form a sailing party on the pond located nearby. At approximately 5:30 p.m. on Monday, April 29, they ventured out. No one knows for sure, but the playful banter led to a challenge, a race to the home of Captain Shepherd, who owned a sailboat and lived on the Post Road (2666 Boston Road), on the north side of the pond.

Gordon Bliss (twenty-eight) and his sister, Asenath (sixteen); Abigail "Nabby" Merrick (sixteen); Mary "Polly" Warriner (sixteen); and Leonard Bliss (twenty-two) all hastened out the back kitchen door by foot except Leonard, who road by horseback ahead of the four. They cross the sun-drench court, through the fields and around the swamp, by an old path to Captain Shepherds. The rest of the party mounted the awaiting horses and took the West Road (Main Street) to the Post Road (Boston Road) where Captain Shepherd lived. Across the road, Shepherd kept his sailboat on the pond, a boat that he built with two masts and sails.

With the sun hanging low in the sky, the party gathered at the pond's edge. Laughter and excitement filled the air as they embarked on their journey. Gordon Bliss, Asenath, Leonard, Abigail "Nabby" Merrick and Mary "Polly" Warriner all took their places. Guy Johnson, a spirited young man from Tolland, Connecticut, joined them. The boat set sail, its canvas wings catching the wind.

The boat danced on the water's surface, playfully racing toward a distant point away from where Captain Shepherd's home stood. The wind toyed with the sails, and the sense of adventure swept them away.

As the boat neared a protruding point of land, fate intervened. A fierce current of wind engulfed them, a force born from the nearby shores. The boat struggled against the elements, swaying perilously. The three young ladies, quick-witted and resourceful, scrambled to the boat's upper side. The boat righted itself, but another gust thrust them into uncertainty. Water engulfed them, and the boat, burdened by the gale, sank beneath the surface.

Desperation hung in the air as friends and bystanders watched from the shore. The wind howled, the waters churned and hearts were gripped with fear. They saw a part of their companions floating for some time on the water. They noticed particularly the red dresses and white bonnets of one or two

Nine Mile Pond in the early 1900s, the area where Captain Shepherd kept his sailboat, 1799. *Atheneum Society of Wilbraham.*

of the young ladies. But whether they sank and rose again, and how often, they could not determine with certainty. They soon, however, lost all hope of their escape. One after another, they all disappeared into the darkness of the water. Nothing was seen except for a solitary hat or two floating on the surface, etching an image that would forever haunt their memories.

As evening descended, hope dwindled and darkness cast its veil. They were overcome by water at about 6:00 p.m. There was no help at hand. The place where they were was difficult to access on account of swamps and brush, and there was no boat short of an adjacent pond. Due to these and other impediments, the bodies all stayed in the water until nearly 8:00 p.m., when Leonard Bliss and Guy Johnson were taken out, followed a short time later by Mary "Polly" Warriner. Even with all remedies resorted to, no signs of returning life appeared.

On the morning of the next day, Gordon Bliss and his sister, Asenath, were found. Gordon had a pocket watch on him the previous day. When his body was discovered, the watch was still keeping perfect time. This watch was presented to the Connecticut River Valley Historical Society back in the 1920s by Mrs. Green.

The bodies of these first five recovered from the waters were brought to the Levi Bliss house, where the gathering was recently held in honor

Nine Mile Pond in 1915, very near the area the tragedy occurred in 1799. *Atheneum Society of Wilbraham.*

of Gordon Bliss. Days of agonizing search followed for Abigail "Nabby" Merrick. The pond yielded no answers, the water clinging to its secrets. The community's grief was palpable, their hearts heavy with loss.

On May 2, the five discovered were interred. Efforts continued to be made for several days by a large body of men with a variety of instruments. At one point, a trench was dug by hand on the west side of the pond in hopes that they could drain it. That effort only brought the water level down a foot, which did not help with the recovery effort.

The midafternoon shadows were lengthening across the fields when the lolling, dust-covered oxen dragged the heavy cannon from the Federal Armory in Springfield onto an elevation west of the pond. Its mighty voice called again and again across the dark waters for the dead to arise. The long reverberations, rolling far away to the south, sounded to the listening dwellers along the mountainside like the tolling of some monster funeral bell for the burial of the Lord. But the sleeper heeded not, nor heard the call, and slept on, undisturbed. The waters were not yet willing to give up their secret. The excitement wore itself away in the general conviction that Abigail "Nabby" Merrick had found her final sepulcher.

On the morning of May 15, after all attempts to recover her bore no fruit, the body of Abigail "Nabby" Merrick was discovered by travelers along the Post Road, drifting before a gentle breeze toward the shore where it had a short time before taking its fatal departure. The scene was heart-wrenching,

The Bliss children's grave, located at Adams Cemetery, Wilbraham, Massachusetts. *David F. Bourcier.*

her features lost to time and water's cruel embrace. She joined her friends in the realm beyond, leaving behind a community forever changed. Abigail was interred the morning after.

The gravestones at Adams Cemetery tell the tale of their lives, a reminder of a tragedy that echoed through time. The boat that had carried their hopes became a somber spectacle, a black-draped reminder of the fragility of life.

In the end, the town's grief found solace in the memory of those lost. Reverend Charles Backus and Reverend Vennilyes presided over their funerals, delivering messages of hope and remembrance. The echoes of that spring day would resonate in Wilbraham's history, a testament to the fleeting nature of life and the strength of a community bound by tragedy.

LOVE, TRAGEDY AND THE PESKY SERPENT

On a scorching August 7, 1761, the air hung heavy with humidity as the sun beat down on the sprawling fields surrounding the small agricultural community named Springfield Mountain. Farmer Lieutenant Thomas Mirick watched his twenty-two-year-old son, Timothy, stride purposefully into the meadow to harvest the hay. The shimmering heat played tricks on the eye, making the distant horizon blur into hazy uncertainty.

Timothy, his scythe glinting in the sunlight, began his task with a mind divided. While his hands moved in practiced arcs, his thoughts were drawn to his beloved, Sarah Lamb, the village sweetheart. The rhythmic swish of the scythe matched the rhythm of his heart, a reminder of his impending wedding just two weeks away.

The meadow where Timothy toiled lay to the southwest of town, a tranquil half-mile stretch that would become forever etched in memory. But this meadow held secrets and contradictions. A debate simmered many decades later regarding its exact location, exacerbated by the division between the neighboring towns of Hampden and Wilbraham.

As the day wore on, the relentless sun painted a scene of serenity. Timothy's thoughts drifted between the sweltering labor and his impending nuptials, little knowing that this day would forever intertwine love, tragedy and the pesky serpent.

In his heart, Timothy believed that he was safe in the embrace of the meadow. However, destiny had a different plan. Hidden within the grasses, a timber rattlesnake slithered, its ominous rattle unheard over the symphony

An 1897 photo. Just beyond this barway was the fatal spot of Timothy Merrick's tragic snakebite in 1761. *Carl Howlett.*

of nature. As Timothy moved, unaware of the danger lurking at his heel, the serpent struck, injecting its deadly venom into the unsuspecting young man.

Hours passed, and as the sun began its descent, Timothy's cries for help went unanswered. His body, bitten and weakening, collapsed onto the earth some distance from the fatal spot and so close to his newly built home. It was a heart-wrenching scene—a young man, so close to beginning a new chapter in his life, laid low by the fangs of an elusive serpent.

The news of Timothy's fate rippled through the tightknit community like a chill wind, casting a shadow over the sons and daughters of the land. This was an era of both unity and isolation, where neighbors were both a helping hand and a distant presence. As the sun dipped below the horizon, the fates of Timothy Mirick and the serpent that took his life became irrevocably linked.

The next day, the farmers embarked on a mission to confront the sinister creature that had caused such sorrow. Their determination matched the weight of their hearts, and it wasn't long before they found the rattlesnake, coiled near the abandoned scythe. It was a symbol of the danger that could so easily befall those who toiled in the fields.

But the story didn't end there. The tale of Timothy's tragedy became interwoven with the essence of local lore. The town's separation, the passing of land through generations and the poignant letters exchanged between betrothed lovers—all became elements in the rich mosaic of history.

In the quaint town of Cold Spring, nestled within the picturesque landscapes of what is now Belchertown, Massachusetts, a tale of love, resilience and enduring legacy unfolds. Two years after the untimely passing of Timothy Mirick, a young and vibrant man with dreams as vast as the

Timothy Merrick's house in the late 1800s. *Wilbraham Public Library.*

horizon, his beloved Sarah Lamb found herself at a crossroads. The memory of Timothy still lingered in her heart, his absence a constant ache. Yet life beckoned her forward, and fate had more in store for her than she could have imagined.

On a crisp winter day, January 19, 1763, Sarah Lamb took a step toward a new chapter in her life. In a charming ceremony that captured the essence of hope and renewal, she married Justus Dwight, a man whose heart was as warm as his spirit was kind. Their union was blessed with the promise of eight children, each a testament to the resilience of love and the fortitude to embrace life's blessings.

Sarah, often described as a woman of indomitable spirit, lived her life with an energy that defied time itself. Her posture remained steadfast, even as the years advanced, and her determination was a beacon for all who knew her. Throughout the passage of time, she and Justus carved out a life together that radiated love, wisdom and enduring companionship.

However, life's journey was not without its challenges. As the years unfurled, Sarah's eyesight dimmed, casting a shadow over her world. Yet her inner light continued to shine brightly, inspiring all who encountered her to persevere and find beauty in life's every facet.

Four years after Timothy's death, the tale of Timothy's unfortunate encounter with a venomous serpent found its way into the pages of Joseph Fisk's remarkable *Ten-Year Almanac*. Fisk's verses breathed life into historical events, painting a vivid tableau of times long gone. His words found their way into households across the thirteen colonies, creating a rich panorama of shared stories that transcended boundaries, but it was the haunting melody of "Springfield Mountain," the folk song that encapsulated Timothy's fate, that truly captured the collective soul of the nation. From humble hearths to bustling taverns, the song echoed through time, its verses shaping a narrative that celebrated both triumph and tragedy. Parodies and variations emerged, adapting to the evolving spirit of the land, until "Springfield Mountain" became a cherished fixture in the annals of traditional American folk songs.

As the years flowed like a river, Sarah Lamb's story and the echoes of Timothy's fate remained intertwined in history. Her legacy, marked by unwavering strength and the power of love's endurance, lived on in the hearts of generations to come. Sarah and Justus found their final resting place in the serene embrace of Dwight Cemetery, a testament to lives well lived and love's enduring embrace.

Fast-forward to the present day, where echoes of that fateful August day still resonate. The descendants of Timothy Mirick carry forward his legacy, alongside their connection to him through the intricate branches of family lineage.

In the quiet of the cemetery, where the new maple trees stand around the old graves, Timothy's memory endures. The story of his life and untimely death lingers, reminding us of the fragile boundary between life and nature's unpredictability. Timothy's spirit lives on, not only in the annals of history but also in the hearts of those who hear his tale, told and retold through generations.

THE UNSPEAKABLE MURDER IN THE HOLLOW OF WILBRAHAM MOUNTAINS

The chilling events of Tuesday, July 26, 1881, on Hampden Road (Hollow Road) in Wilbraham cast a dark shadow over the small community. The lifeless body of Rueben S. Cadwell, a seventy-three-year-old town pauper residing with Cyrus Day of Monson, was discovered the following Wednesday evening by two men passing through a nearby pasture.

Cadwell, known for undertaking side jobs for Mr. Day, met a gruesome end. His face and head bore brutal bruising, while the marks of strangulation on his throat painted a horrifying picture. The location of his body, under a fence in a pasture south of Moses Hancock Jr.'s house, added an eerie element to the tragedy.

The events leading to Cadwell's demise centered on a task to drive a cow to the Hampden Road pasture. Morris Monihan, described as a shiftless and dirty individual employed by Mr. Day, accompanied Cadwell. However, Monihan returned alone to Mr. Day's home in Monson, claiming that Cadwell had ventured in another direction.

An autopsy conducted by Dr. Holbrook of Palmer unveiled a fractured skull behind Cadwell's right ear, but the cause of death was determined to be choking. The windpipe had been so violently compressed that it was torn and disfigured. The body's advanced decomposition necessitated immediate burial.

Suspicion fell on Morris Monihan, leading to his arrest. Despite loud conversations reportedly overheard between the two men after their pasture visit, Monihan vehemently denied any knowledge of the murder. However,

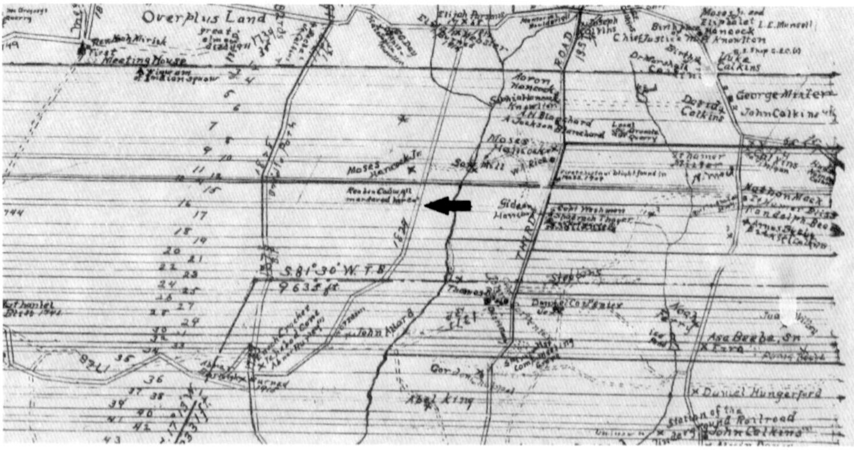

The arrow on this 1917 map from Henry Edson indicates the site of the Rueben S. Cadwell murder. *Atheneum Society of Wilbraham.*

the case took an unexpected turn in December 1881 when Monihan was indicted for manslaughter by the grand jury of Springfield.

In a surprising twist, Judge Wells declared Monihan insane, redirecting the course of justice. The accused was subsequently committed to the New Hampshire Asylum for the Insane. This turn of events not only highlights the brutality of the crime but also raises questions about Monihan's mental state at the time.

The historical narrative serves as a poignant reminder of the complexities surrounding investigations and justice in the late nineteenth century. The commitment of Monihan to an asylum suggests a recognition, albeit limited, of mental health considerations during that period. The mysteries and tragic end of Rueben S. Cadwell continue to linger in the annals of history, a haunting reminder of the challenges faced by communities in times long past.

ABRAHAM AVERY III AND HIS DEVIOUS SADDLE

Abraham Avery III made his way to Wilbraham from the Montville, Connecticut area in the early 1800s. He settled at 239 Main Street in a home built circa 1785, although the previous occupants remain unknown.

His first wife, Elizabeth Bliss Avery, hailed from a prestigious Wilbraham family and was born on January 29, 1788, to Abel Bliss Jr. Her family's prominence in North Wilbraham's high society was evident. Elizabeth's childhood was marked by a tragic event on April 29, 1799, when three cousins and three others drowned in Nine Mile Pond during a family celebration at her uncle's house.

On February 20, 1810, Elizabeth gave birth to their first child, Addison Avery. However, subsequent years brought heartbreak with the early deaths of their next four children: an infant (one day old), Benjamin (six years old), Simeon (one year old) and Elizabeth (eighteen years old). Two other children who were born and survived were Julia Avery Rand and Abraham Avery IV.

Abraham Avery III—a skilled tanner, saddler and harness maker—gained a reputation as the best in the region. His harness shop, located about five hundred feet south of his home at 267 Main Street, showcased his craftsmanship. The building, originally built circa 1790, still stands today as a private residence. The tanning vats for his shop were likely situated at the rear of the property, benefiting from the nearby stream.

A prominent figure in town, Abraham was not only a successful businessman but also a devoted Methodist. He played a key role in founding the Wesleyan Academy at Wilbraham and Wesleyan University at Middletown, Connecticut. Additionally, he served as a trustee and represented Wilbraham in the state legislature.

Portrait of Abraham Avery. *Wood engraving by W.B. Closson.*

The rivalry between the Methodist and Orthodox denominations became evident when the tax collector demanded payment from Abraham for the support of the Orthodox church. Known for his cunning and love for practical jokes, Abraham decided to turn the tables on the tax collector. He hatched a plan that combined his skilled craftsmanship with a mischievous twist. Crafting a saddle that outwardly resembled a masterpiece fit for royalty, Abraham knew that it lacked the structural integrity beneath its shiny façade.

Days later, the tax collector returned with the constable, demanding payment once again. Little did they know that Abraham had strategically left the questionable saddle in plain view. The tax collector's attention shifted to the splendid creation before him, and he demanded it as payment. With a scoff, Abraham acquiesced, "Take it then."

As the constable loaded the saddle into his wagon, little did they realize that they were unwittingly becoming accomplices in Abraham's clever scheme. The saddle fetched a handsome price at auction, far surpassing the owed tax. Surprisingly, the constable offered the surplus to Abraham, who, true to his principles, refused both the excess money and the gold offered in compensation.

The saddle found a new owner, an eager gentleman from Belchertown. Excited to showcase his prized purchase, he mounted his horse. However, as he rode off, the saddle began to unravel, piece by piece. Frustrated and angered, the gentleman went to Abraham's shop, demanding accountability.

With a twinkle in his eye, Abraham feigned innocence. "Ah," he quipped, "that's the Presbyterian saddle. I have nothing to do with that." The gentleman, though furious, couldn't help but appreciate Abraham's wit.

This tale passed down through generations, becoming a legendary example of wit triumphing over adversity. Abraham's ability to navigate challenges with humor and resourcefulness made him a local hero, and his leather shop continued to thrive with a reputation for both quality craftsmanship and clever pranks.

Elizabeth's childhood home at 288 Main Street. *Wilbraham Public Library.*

Abraham's first wife, Elizabeth, passed away on December 27, 1851, at the age of sixty-three. He later married Cordelia Belinda Brewer, who outlived him by twenty-three years. Abraham Avery III passed away on October 8, 1853, at the age of seventy-one. They are all interred at Woodland Dell Cemetery in Wilbraham, leaving behind a legacy of craftsmanship, wit and community involvement.

THE WILBRAHAM MEN WHO HELPED SAVE THE FEDERAL ARMORY

In the quiet town of Wilbraham, where the winter air hung heavy with tension and discontent, a group of courageous residents found themselves at the forefront of an unexpected historical event: Shays's Rebellion. As the winds of rebellion blew through the region, the people of Wilbraham played a pivotal role in thwarting Daniel Shays's audacious plan to attack the Federal Armory.

On January 24, 1787, Shays arrived in Wilbraham during the afternoon with the intention of lodging his soldiers overnight with the local inhabitants, including along the old abandoned road along Twelve Mile Brook.

Shays dispatched a picket of four men to inspect a nearby house on West Road belonging to Deacon Noah Warriner, ensuring that it was safe for an overnight stay. Upon arrival, they encountered a locked door to the north-front second-floor bedroom chamber. Disturbed by the sounds within, their attempts to gain entry were met with silence. Frustrated, one of them proposed, "Let's smoke him out!" The idea gained unanimous approval, leading them to climb onto the roof. They strategically covered the north flue of the chimney with a damp blanket, intensifying the fire downstairs, and hastened back to the locked chamber.

As the flames roared below, smoke billowed through the fireplace into the room above, creating a stifling atmosphere. To their surprise, the locked door burst open, revealing not a mysterious figure but a distressed woman. She clutched a baby of about six months old, emerging from the smoke-filled chamber in distress, coughing and gasping for air. The unconventional method had indeed "smoked them out," although the outcome differed significantly from the men's initial expectations.

It could be possible that this woman's act was part of a greater plan to keep those men of Shays engaged around the Warriner house while Deputy Sheriff Asaph King, Colonel Abel King, Deacon Noah Warriner and his next-door neighbor Dr. Samuel Merrick were holding their conference in a nearby house, most likely Dr. Samuel Merrick's, to arrange a way to inform General Shepard of Shays's plan on attacking the Federal Armory.

The insurgents were strategically divided into three main groups to encircle and launch a simultaneous attack on the armory. Shays commanded one contingent positioned east in Wilbraham, while Luke Day led a second force located across the Connecticut River in West Springfield. Eli Parsons led a third force positioned to the north at Chicopee. Originally, the rebels had planned their assault for January 25. However, at the eleventh hour, Day changed the date and informed Shays that the attack would be delayed until the twenty-sixth. Unfortunately for Shays and Parsons, Day's message was intercepted.

Fate took an unexpected turn as the rebel messenger, braving the biting cold, sought refuge in a Springfield tavern to ward off the chill. Unbeknownst to him, a group of astute young men at the tavern, sensing a clandestine plot, hospitably plied the messenger with drinks until he succumbed to a drunken slumber. Seizing the opportunity, they skillfully retrieved Day's letter from the messenger's pocket.

However, a more dire fate awaited Shays and his followers. The residents of Wilbraham were not idle in the face of the approaching force. Asaph King, then deputy sheriff, along with Colonel Abel King, Dr. Samuel F. Merrick and Deacon Noah Warriner, convened to devise a plan to alert General Shepard about the imminent threat. Ultimately, it was decided that the responsibility fell on the sheriff.

On the morning of the twenty-fifth, as Shays advanced toward Springfield along the Bay Road, Sheriff King mounted a splendid young horse waiting in his barn. Navigating through fields and overcoming obstacles such as knee-deep snow and crusty terrain, he reached West Street (Stony Hill Road). From there he continued west. The journey took a toll on his horse, its legs streaming with blood upon emerging onto the Bay Road. Despite the challenges, King managed to reach the arsenal in just forty-five minutes from leaving Wilbraham.

With King's timely arrival, General Shepard learned crucial details about the size and proximity of Shays's force, enabling him to prepare for the impending confrontation. The weather delayed Shays, who only appeared on the road around four o'clock in the afternoon.

Consequently, on the twenty-fifth, as Shays's and Parsons's militias approached the armory, they were unaware that they would receive no support from the west. Instead, they encountered Shepard's militia lying in wait. Shepard initially ordered warning shots to be fired over the heads of Shays's men, followed by the discharge of grapeshot from two cannons. This action resulted in the death of four Shaysites and the wounding of twenty others. Remarkably, there was no exchange of musket fire between the opposing forces. The collapse of the rebel advance led to most of the insurgent forces fleeing northward. Shays's forces scattered and fled to Ludlow, where they spent the night. Eventually, both Shays's and Day's forces regrouped in Amherst, Massachusetts.

Stories circulated of John Langdon, a veteran of two wars in Shepard's army, recounting how he, with his "Queen's Ann" at the ready, intimidated a squad of Shays's men into surrendering. Despite rumors of a few Wilbraham men in Shays's mob, many from the town stood with General Shepard. Notably, nine Chaffees answered the roll call on the morning of the battle, their names causing amusement: Asa Chaffee, Asa Chaffee Jr., Comfort Chaffee, Comfort Chaffee Jr. and so on. Reports also suggest that near Sessions's place, four or five individuals from the south part of the town, on their way to join the insurgents, were informed of Shays's defeat by someone returning from the conflict, signaling that "it is all over."

Four thousand individuals admitted their involvement in the rebellion by signing confessions in exchange for amnesty. Although several hundred participants faced indictments related to the rebellion, the majority of them were pardoned under a broad amnesty, with only a few key leaders excluded. While eighteen men were initially convicted and sentenced to death, many of

Image of Shays's Rebellion, 1786. *Libcom.org*

these sentences were commuted or overturned on appeal or the individuals were ultimately pardoned.

Daniel Shays himself was granted a pardon in 1788, leading to his return to Massachusetts from hiding in the Vermont wilderness. He faced significant vilification from the Boston press, which portrayed him as an emblematic anarchist who opposed the government. Later, he relocated to the Conesus area of New York, where he lived out the remainder of his life in poverty and obscurity, passing away in 1825.

VICTORY'S ASCENT

THE 1908 WILBRAHAM MOUNTAIN CHALLENGE

On Friday, September 11, 1908, the small town of Wilbraham buzzed with excitement as the sun rose over the mountains, casting a golden hue on the rolling hills that framed the horizon. The air was electric with anticipation as townsfolk and visitors alike gathered along Monson Road, eagerly awaiting the historic hill climb race about to unfold.

Organized under the auspices of the prestigious Springfield Automobile Club and proudly sponsored by the Automobile Club of Massachusetts, this event was more than just a race—it was a celebration of innovation, engineering prowess and the relentless spirit of adventure that defined the Brass Era of automotive manufacturing.

The seventy-two-car field was meticulously organized into twenty-one distinct classes, carefully considering engine type, displacement and price ranges to ensure fairness and competitiveness. Additionally, a modified class was established to accommodate vehicles with customized enhancements, further diversifying the competition. Furthermore, to celebrate the diversity of motorcycling, dedicated classes were designated to showcase the unique capabilities of motorcycles.

The challenging one-mile course traversed up Monson Road, with the starting line positioned roughly 500 feet east of Main Street. The course culminated just before reaching Ridge Road, offering competitors a demanding ascent from an elevation of 300 feet to 770 feet. With the steepest grade of 23 percent, the course demanded skill and precision from drivers navigating its twists and turns. Despite the formidable terrain, the average grade of 8.5 percent ensured a thrilling yet manageable competition. The natural hardness and firmness of the dirt road added to the intensity of the race, requiring drivers to exhibit both finesse and agility. Each car was meticulously timed over the measured mile by the esteemed Timing Club of New York City, ensuring accuracy and fairness in determining the victors of this exhilarating event.

In the past, Monson Road, with its rugged terrain and challenging ascent, emerged as an unofficial proving ground for the daring engineers and manufacturers of automobiles and motorcycles in the Springfield area.

The automobile club secured the road for a generous four-day period preceding the hill climb event, affording participants ample time for practice runs to familiarize themselves with the challenging course. Additionally, meticulous preparations were undertaken to ensure optimal conditions for both drivers and spectators. All rocks were diligently removed from the road surface to guarantee a smooth and safe racing environment. Moreover, a grandstand was erected near the point of the steepest grade, providing spectators with an unrivaled vantage point to witness the entirety of the thrilling racecourse.

As the clock ticked closer to the starting time, the streets thrummed with the rumble of engines and the gleam of polished brass fixtures catching the sunlight. Drivers clad in leather goggles and dashing caps exchanged nods and smiles, their camaraderie tinged with the competitive edge that fueled their passion for speed.

Twenty thrilling events were meticulously planned, attracting approximately seventy formidable "machines" eager to showcase their prowess on the challenging terrain. Among the prestigious car manufacturers competing were Stevens-Duryea, Knox, Buick, Chalmers, Cameron, Middleby, Jackson, Bailey, Atlas and Stanley Steamer, each bringing its finest vehicles to vie for victory.

Ultimately, it was the Stevens-Duryea, crafted in Chicopee Falls, and the Knox Automobile Company's offering from Springfield that emerged as the show winners. Piloted by the skilled Charles Basle, the winning Knox Giant blazed through the arduous dirt road mile in a remarkable one minute and eight seconds, achieving an astonishing average speed of 52.9 miles per hour. Basle's performance not only secured the victory but also set the record for the fastest time recorded by an automobile throughout the entire meet.

Meanwhile, the Indian Motorcycle proved its mettle by completing the challenging course in a swift one minute and three-fifths of a second, further

Knox Giant, piloted by the skilled Charles Basle. *Wilbraham Public Library.*

highlighting the impressive capabilities of these powerful machines in navigating the demanding terrain.

The scene along Monson Road was nothing short of spectacular, with approximately eight hundred automobiles lining the course and an impressive crowd of between five and six thousand spectators gathered to witness the thrilling events unfold. Despite the adrenaline-fueled excitement, the day remained largely safe, with only one reported racing accident. Peter Robinson, navigating a Stevens-Duryea, encountered a mishap as the vehicle rolled over, resulting in its complete wreckage. Miraculously, Robinson escaped with only a broken leg.

The Monson Road course, renowned as "the toughest climb in New England," lived up to its reputation, offering competitors and spectators alike a true test of skill and endurance. The presence of a treacherous "switchback" curve, situated in front of what is now 220 Monson Road, added an extra layer of challenge to the already demanding ascent. This iconic feature further solidified Monson Road's status as a legendary battleground for automotive enthusiasts, leaving an indelible mark on the annals of motorsport history.

The historic hill climb race of September 11, 1908, would be remembered as more than just a sporting event—it was a testament to the indomitable spirit of a generation captivated by the promise of the open road, where brass gleamed brightly against the backdrop of a changing world. As the sun set on Wilbraham that evening, it cast its final rays on a legacy that would endure for generations to come.

In the early 1900s, the town of Wilbraham found itself at the forefront of an automotive revolution, as pioneers like Henry W. Cutler and Fred R. Collins embraced the burgeoning world of horseless carriages. With their visionary spirit and a taste for adventure, they paved the way for a new era of transportation that would forever transform the landscape of their community.

Among the notable vehicles gracing the streets of Wilbraham were the illustrious 1905 Knox touring car owned by Henry W. Cutler and the sleek 1905 Cadillac belonging to Fred R. Collins. These marvels of engineering captured the imagination of townsfolk and visitors alike, their gleaming brass fittings and polished exteriors symbolizing the dawn of a modern age.

As word of these remarkable automobiles spread, Wilbraham experienced a surge in automotive enthusiasm. By 1913, the once-sleepy town boasted an estimated thirty to forty automobiles, each representing a triumph of innovation and a testament to the pioneering spirit that thrived within its borders. The streets that once echoed with the *clip-clop* of horse hooves now reverberated with the hum of engines and the excited chatter of onlookers as residents marveled at the sight of these modern marvels traversing their familiar roads.

In 2013, the town of Wilbraham embarked on a journey to honor its rich automotive history by commemorating the iconic 1908 hill climb event during its 250th anniversary celebrations. The reenactment captured the imagination of the community and beyond, drawing enthusiasts from far and wide to witness a piece of living history. The success of this inaugural reenactment paved the way for subsequent events in 2015 and 2017, each one growing in popularity and scope as antique car and motorcycle enthusiasts flocked to participate.

Unfortunately, the much-anticipated 2020 event faced an unexpected hurdle with its cancelation due to the global pandemic. However, the spirit of the Wilbraham Hill Climb refused to be extinguished, and in 2023, the event made a triumphant return, marking a new chapter in its storied legacy. On Saturday, May 13, 2023, the hills of Wilbraham echoed once again with the roar of vintage engines as the reinvigorated event showcased a spectacular array of pre–World War II cars, driven by members of the Vintage Sports Car Club of America. Spectators lined the route, their eyes alight with nostalgia as they watched these meticulously restored vehicles navigate the challenging course with grace and precision.

The original 1956 dedication plaque commemorating the 1906 Wilbraham Mountain Hill Climb, now displayed at the Wilbraham Town Hall. *David F. Bourcier.*

The atmosphere crackled with excitement as enthusiasts mingled, swapping stories and sharing their passion for automotive history. Amid the throng of spectators, one notable figure stood out: Wayne Carini, star of *Chasing Classic Cars*, made a special appearance, adding an extra layer of prestige to the event and further cementing its status as a must-attend affair for vintage car aficionados.

THE RUMORS OF CAPTAIN KIDD'S GOLD

Around 1850, persistent rumors circulated in numerous New England towns suggesting that portions of "Captain Kidd's gold" lay buried within their borders. In Wilbraham during this era, one particular individual harbored a firm belief—or perhaps a fantastical dream—that some of this legendary treasure was concealed atop our local mountain. Specifically, he envisioned its presence within an ancient cellar hole situated on the eastern slope of Ridge Road, just north of the present-day intersection with Monson Road.

Captain William Kidd (circa 1645–1701) was a Scottish privateer turned pirate who gained legendary status despite capturing only one significant prize ship. Persistent rumors suggest that he buried a vast treasure that remains undiscovered. Kidd's downfall began with his arrest in Boston in July 1699 and continued when he was brought to England in April 1700. In 1701, he met his end at Wapping Old Stairs, located on the southern bank of the Thames, beyond London Bridge and the Tower of London, at the infamous Execution Dock.

Pirates meeting their grisly fate at Execution Dock faced an unsettling end. The gallows there were infamous for employing a short drop method, which meant that the condemned pirates were not killed instantly by a broken neck but instead slowly strangled. This caused their bodies to convulse and twitch, giving the appearance of a macabre dance as they died.

Captain William Kidd, one of the most infamous pirates of his time, met his end in this manner in 1701. His body was gibbeted and left suspended in the Thames estuary for three years, serving as a haunting symbol of the consequences of this crime during the Golden Age of Piracy.

Before his arrival in Boston, Captain William Kidd took precautions to bury his stolen treasure, with potential locations including New Jersey, Long Island and Gardiners Island. Under pressure from authorities in Boston, Kidd disclosed some of these hiding spots. He was compelled to provide a detailed inventory of his loot, which survives as a historical document today. Among the recovered items listed were silver ingots, gold coins, jewels, bales of silk and substantial quantities of iron and sugar.

Despite this disclosure, a legend persisted that Kidd had not revealed all of his treasure. It was believed that another cache, possibly larger than the recovered loot, remained hidden somewhere. This tantalizing legend fueled centuries of treasure-hunting endeavors in locations remotely associated with Captain Kidd, all without success. The speculation about the treasure's whereabouts ranged from the eastern coast of America to as far as India.

While the actual existence of undiscovered treasure remains a mystery, Kidd's penchant for burying loot has firmly entrenched itself in pirate folklore and fiction. His story and the search for his hidden treasure have become integral parts of pirate tales and continue to capture imaginations to this day.

Others in Wilbraham during the 1850s became intrigued by the rumors of Captain Kidd's buried gold, prompting them to embark on nocturnal expeditions to the site. Night after night, they diligently dug into the earth around the old cellar, hoping to uncover the hidden treasure. According to local belief, absolute silence was crucial during these excavations. It was feared that if the iron case containing the gold was unearthed and the tranquility of the night was disturbed by a human voice, the treasure would mysteriously vanish, sinking deep into the mountain's depths beyond reach.

Portrait of Captain Kidd. *From the* Courier Evening Telegraph.

Among the curious onlookers was a young boy, about eight or ten years old, eager to unravel the mystery like many boys his age. He stealthily followed the men with their picks and shovels from his home late in the evening to the deserted cellar, maintaining a cautious distance to observe their activities unnoticed. Remarkably, he survived the eerie experience and later recounted the incident to Chauncey Peck, the author of the 1913 *History of Wilbraham*.

During the time of Captain Kidd, the area now known as Wilbraham was referred to as the Outward Commons, predominantly known as Springfield Mountain. This region was largely wilderness and remained unsettled at that time. The only road in the area was the Bay Path, which connected the settlement of Springfield to the town of Boston. The rumored location of Kidd's treasure was about two miles south of this road, along the ridge of the mountain. It is highly unlikely that Captain Kidd hid any treasure there, especially considering that the supposed old foundation where the treasure was hidden likely did not exist during his era. However, this notion makes for an intriguing fictional story about Captain Kidd and his hidden plunder.

THE ELECTRIC RAILWAY IN NORTH WILBRAHAM

The expansion of trolley lines into smaller towns and communities played a crucial role in connecting people, facilitating commerce and contributing to the overall growth and development of these areas. The convenience and accessibility provided by trolley systems were instrumental in shaping the way people traveled and interacted with their surroundings during that period.

Understanding the widespread reach of trolley systems helps paint a more comprehensive picture of how public transportation infrastructure evolved and adapted to the needs of both urban and rural populations in the late nineteenth and early twentieth centuries. It's a fascinating aspect of history that showcases the interconnectedness of communities through innovative transportation solutions.

The transition from horse-drawn trolleys to electric motor cars in Springfield, Massachusetts, during the late nineteenth century marked a significant advancement in transportation technology. In March 1870, the introduction of the first horse-drawn trolley, running on rails, represented an early form of public transportation in Springfield.

However, by 1890, a major shift had occurred as part of the trolley system was upgraded to electric motor cars. The adoption of electric technology in the transportation sector was a transformative development during that era. Electric-powered trolleys offered several advantages over their horse-drawn counterparts, including increased speed and efficiency and reduced reliance on animal power.

The rapid discontinuation of horse-drawn trolleys in favor of electric motor cars highlights the efficiency and popularity of electric propulsion in urban transportation. This transition mirrored a broader trend in many cities and regions during the late nineteenth and early twentieth centuries, as electric power became more widely available and practical for various applications, including public transportation.

The extension of trolley lines from the core of the city into the outskirts, including the near Wilbraham town line at the Putts Bridge in Indian Orchard, indicates the expanding reach and influence of the Springfield Street Railway in the late nineteenth century.

The efforts made by Wilbraham to have the trolley line extended through North Wilbraham, even though initially unsuccessful, demonstrate the community's interest in integrating with the expanding transportation network. The eventual success in extending trolley service to North Wilbraham on September 17, 1901, was achieved through the involvement of the Palmer and Monson Street Railway.

The granting of a franchise to the Palmer and Monson Street Railway, later succeeded by the Springfield and Eastern Street Railway in 1906, allowed for the operation of the trolley through the north end of Wilbraham. This connection also facilitated the integration of the eastern terminus of the Springfield Street Railway system at the Putts Bridge in Indian Orchard.

The extension of the trolley service to North Wilbraham from the east marked a significant development in the accessibility and connectivity of the region, providing residents with an efficient means of transportation and contributing to the overall growth and development of the area.

The efforts made by the residents of Wilbraham in February 1912 to further extend the trolley line reflect the community's continued interest in expanding and enhancing its transportation infrastructure. The proposal, presented as a warrant article at the town meeting, aimed to extend the trolley line in Springfield from Wilbraham Road by Watershops Pond, through Sixteen Acres, along Springfield Street to the center village and then on to North Wilbraham to connect with the existing trolley system.

Although the warrant article successfully passed the town meeting, indicating local support for the expansion, the proposal to the Springfield and Eastern Street Railway Company did not lead to success. It's not uncommon for various challenges—such as financial constraints, logistical issues or differing priorities—to hinder the implementation of such plans.

The dynamics of negotiating with transportation companies and coordinating the expansion of trolley lines could be complex. Despite the setback, the initial support from the town meeting indicates a strong desire within the community for improved connectivity and accessibility through an extended trolley network.

The tracing of the trolley route from Indian Orchard, heading on Stony Hill Road to Old Boston Road and crossing the dry bridge (Moran's Bridge) over the railroad tracks, indicates the careful planning and engineering involved in establishing the trolley line. Traveling along Boston Road, passing through Collins Depot and crossing under the railroad bridge showcases the integration of the trolley system with existing transportation infrastructure.

The deviation from Boston Road at Silver Street, where the trolley traveled through the woods on the north side of the railroad tracks into Palmer, enabled the line to run parallel to the tracks while maintaining a flatter and more manageable grade. The remnants of the old trolley bed and stone bridges that passed over many streams still exist in the area today, serving as tangible remnants of this historical mode of transportation.

Understanding the specific details of the trolley route provides a unique perspective on how communities were connected and how transportation networks were established in the past. It's a testament to the engineering and planning efforts of that time, leaving behind traces that continue to shape the landscape and history of the region.

The electrification of the entire trolley line between Springfield and Worcester by 1907 marked a significant milestone in the development of electrically operated passenger transportation in New England. This electrification process was part of a broader trend in the early twentieth century to transition from horse-drawn and steam-powered systems to electrically powered ones, providing more efficient and reliable services. The completion of electrification made the trolley line between Springfield and

Trolly tracks along the river "Dug Way" in 1908. *Wilbraham Public Library.*

Worcester, Massachusetts, the longest electrically operated passenger trolley line in New England at that time.

Having an electrified trolley line connecting major cities like Springfield and Worcester would have had a substantial impact on regional mobility, facilitating faster and more convenient travel for passengers. The electrification of such extensive trolley lines played a pivotal role in shaping the landscape of public transportation during the early twentieth century, providing a model for efficient and electrified transit systems that would later become more widespread.

The utilization of the trolley system by town residents, including high school students and those with businesses in Springfield, reflected the convenience and flexibility that this mode of travel offered during that period. The ability to ride to North Wilbraham by horse and carriage and then switch to the trolley for transportation to Springfield provided a practical and efficient solution for daily commuting.

Stabling the horse for the day at Collins Livery while taking advantage of the trolley for travel to and from Springfield highlights a combination of traditional transportation methods and the emerging electric trolley system. This approach allowed individuals to benefit from the speed and efficiency of the trolley for the longer part of their journey while still relying on traditional means for the initial and final legs of the commute.

It's a fascinating glimpse into the daily routines and practical considerations that shaped the choices people made in navigating their communities and accessing neighboring towns.

The transition from trolleys to buses in 1928 marked a significant shift in the mode of public transportation in the north end of Wilbraham. The decision to convert to buses and the granting of a franchise to the Springfield

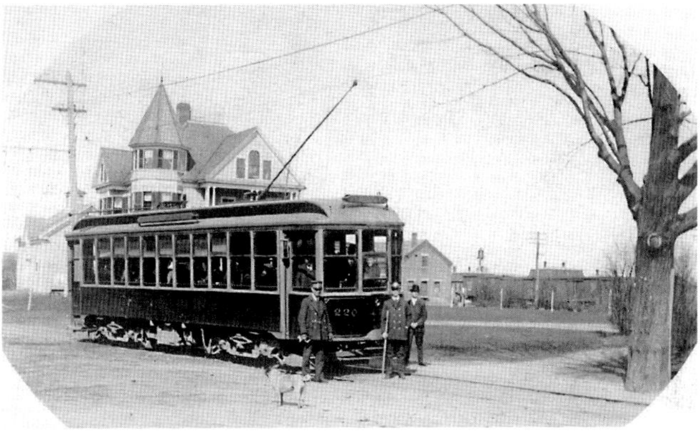

Car 220 coming from Palmer and heading to Indian Orchard, early 1900s. This scheduled stop is in North Wilbraham at the Railroad Depot. *Wilbraham Public Library.*

Street Railway to operate buses from Indian Orchard to North Wilbraham underscored the changing landscape of transportation.

The abandonment of the old trolley tracks signified the end of an era and the beginning of a new phase in the town's public transportation history. The introduction of buses likely brought about advantages such as increased flexibility in routes and reduced maintenance costs compared to the infrastructure required for trolley tracks.

This shift from trolleys to buses was part of a broader trend in the early to mid-twentieth century, where many communities transitioned to bus systems as a more versatile and cost-effective means of providing public transportation. The decision to make this change in Wilbraham reflects the evolving nature of transportation technology and the need to adapt to the changing preferences and demands of the community.

SPECTRAL JUSTICE

UNRAVELING THE MARCUS LYON MURDER AND THE DUAL DESCENT TO THE GALLOWS

In the serene backdrop of Wilbraham in the fall of 1805, the peaceful town was shattered by the grim events surrounding the untimely demise of Marcus Lyon. This historical narrative, layered with intrigue and prejudice, unveils a poignant tale of justice and societal biases during a time when Irish immigrants faced suspicion and hostility.

It all began on that fateful Saturday, November 9, when a neighbor of John Bliss discovered a horse grazing in John's mowing lot, seemingly abandoned. John sent a boy to bring the horse to the house, where it was tied in hopes that the owner would return. One theory was that a local doctor, known for leaving his horse untied to graze while visiting a friend or patient, might have been in the neighborhood at the time, and the horse consequently wandered off.

The day took an ominous turn when the horse, saddled and bridled, couldn't be claimed by any local resident. As the cloudy afternoon unfolded, the town's sense of normalcy crumbled. As nightfall came, some information was gleaned and that the horse was ridden by a stranger to the east on Boston Post Road, about two hours before the horse was first discovered in the mowing lot of John Bliss. Suspicion now arose that the horse was stolen and that the person had abandoned it to make their escape, but this suspicion appeared not altogether consistent.

On the next day, as the sun dipped into the afternoon sky, a decision was made to delve into the contents of the mysterious saddlebags. A palpable

The mowing lot of John Bliss, as it looks today. *David F. Bourcier.*

sense of anticipation hung in the air, fueled by the hope that hidden clues might unravel the enigma at hand.

Upon careful examination, a trove of intriguing items was unveiled. Plain articles of apparel, a well-worn pair of shoes and more than half a dozen letters addressed to gentlemen in Monson, Palmer and Woodstock, Connecticut, surfaced. All signs pointed to a man named Marcus Lyon, a twenty-three-year-old from Woodstock who had recently been working in Cazenovia, New York, as the owner of these possessions.

The intrigue deepened when one of the letters was found to be open, revealing a crucial date: November 4, 1805. The ink-stained letter bore the location of Cazenovia, New York. It was a pivotal piece of evidence that thrust the gathered individuals into a whirlwind of speculation. Whispers spread like wildfire through the community, weaving a tale that Marcus Lyon was the mysterious horseman. The pieces of the puzzle seemed to be falling into place, and the revelation sent ripples of curiosity and suspicion among those who sought to uncover the truth behind this captivating mystery.

As suspicions deepened, a sinister undertone crept into the narrative of the young man's disappearance, suggesting the possibility of foul play.

With a sense of urgency, a search party assembled on that ominous Sunday afternoon, combing through the landscape in a quest for answers.

The investigation led them to the shores of the Chicopee River, where the water whispered secrets of potential tragedy. Every rustle in the adjoining woods held a promise of revelation, and each hidden nook was scrutinized for any sign that might reveal the fate of the unfortunate soul.

The search extended to places deemed likely to conceal the remains of the mysterious victim, yet the landscape held its secrets tightly. Despite the collective efforts, the late afternoon sun dipped below the horizon, casting long shadows over the unresolved mystery. No discovery was made, leaving the search party with more questions than answers; a cloud of uncertainty hung over the unsettling circumstances surrounding the young man's disappearance.

The unfolding mystery took an intriguing turn as a crucial witness, thirteen-year-old Laertes Fuller, stepped into the spotlight. Son of Abraham Fuller, young Laertes disclosed a pivotal encounter that transpired on the fateful Saturday, just past noon, as he tended to his duties of driving swine to the mountain.

In the midst of his pastoral task, Laertes stumbled on a puzzling scene near the stone bridge that spanned Spear Brook. Two figures, one of whom he later unequivocally identified following their subsequent arrest, were leading a horse westward from the bridge's vicinity. Their actions shrouded in secrecy, they engaged in what appeared to be a hasty and clandestine conversation.

Laertes keenly observed as one of the men, wielding a bludgeon, deftly prodded the horse forward, while the other maintained a firm grip on the bridle. The mysterious duo swiftly veered from the main road onto the high road, specifically the 1732 Old Bay Path, ultimately leading to the location where the horse would later be discovered.

Sensing the peculiarity of the situation, Laertes couldn't resist his youthful curiosity and discreetly trailed the men up the hill. The unfolding drama reached a dramatic pause as the men paused, exchanged furtive words and noticed the young observer. Abruptly, one of them mounted the horse, galloping up the mountain and disappearing from view, while the other lingered, leaning against a stone wall with an intense gaze fixed on the boy.

Undeterred, Laertes continued a few yards past the wall, plucked some apples from an adjacent tree and made his way home in the opposite direction. Throughout this escapade, the stranger's watchful eyes followed the boy until he vanished from sight. The stage was set for a narrative laden with intrigue, leaving the community on edge, desperate for answers to the enigma.

Laertes Fuller's account took a more ominous turn as he revealed a previous sighting of the same two men on foot, heading from the east toward the area in question, a mere fifteen minutes before the horse-related incident. This unsettling revelation unfolded in the evening's darkness, around 160 yards away from where the men were later observed with the horse.

Undeterred by the encroaching night, the search party pressed on, aided by the feeble glow of torches and lanterns. Despite their determined efforts, the shadows cast by the night hid any trace of the mysterious events that had transpired. As darkness clung to the surroundings, a collective decision was reached to suspend the search until the light of day could aid their efforts.

However, just as the search appeared to be winding down, a new and alarming circumstance emerged, reigniting the resolve of those involved. This new information was about a young man, passing by on Sunday, who had stumbled upon the remnants of a shattered pistol guard and a pistol ramrod just a few feet west of where the two mysterious men were first seen with the horse. This discovery fueled a growing conviction among those involved in the investigation that they were on the brink of uncovering a potential crime.

Eager to unveil the truth, the search party prepared for another round of investigation, setting the stage for a night fraught with anticipation and an unsettling mystery that begged to be unraveled. With a sense of dread hanging in the air, a decision was reached to conduct a thorough search in the vicinity—among the bushes and along the riverbank just west of where Spear Brook enters the river. The belief that the remains of a man might be found not far from where the pistol parts were discovered intensified the search.

As nightfall descended, several gentlemen, armed with lights, ventured to the spot where the broken pistol pieces had been found. The bushes were meticulously examined but yielded no results. Attention then turned to the riverbank, with a focus on a shallow area where it was initially thought the crime may have occurred. However, the search proved futile.

Undeterred, the group redirected their efforts downstream, to a bowed section of the river occasionally used as a bathing place. In this darkened landscape, illuminated by torchlight, M.K. Bartlett and P. Bliss made a crucial discovery. Mr. Bartlett saw something in the water that caught his eye, and while he was looking, before he had time to conclude and speak, Mr. Bliss picked up a pistol close to Mr. Bartlett's feet, which was broken, with blood

View of 2957 Boston Road, the site of the Marcus Lyon murder in 1805, as it appears today. *David F. Bourcier.*

and hair on it, and said, "The man is not far from here." The alarm was instantly given, and those who were out on the search soon drew near. They saw the body, lying on its face, with the feet out from the shore and the head close to the land, in the depth of water but a few inches more than sufficient to cover it. The greatcoat on the body was gathered in a careless fold and laid on the back side of the head, with a stone placed thereon, partly out of water. There was the appearance of a body having been dragged from the road to this place through mud, grass and more.

Following careful consideration, the unsettling decision was made to remove the lifeless body from the water, sparing it from its shocking aquatic grave until the arrival of the coroner's inquest, which was not scheduled until the following day. Recognizing the solemnity of the situation, and perhaps out of a sense of respect for the deceased, it was deemed more fitting to expedite the process.

A wagon was promptly secured for this somber purpose. In the presence of those who would bear witness to the macabre evidence, the mangled remains of a fellow citizen were delicately lifted from the water. The silent conveyance of the tragic figure commenced, winding through the night to reach a more fitting resting place.

The destination was Sykes Tavern, situated at the northwest corner of Maple and Chapel Streets and operated by Mr. Asa Caulkins. The establishment, familiar to many in the community, now bore the weight of a sorrowful secret—a grim testament to the unfolding tragedy that had cast its shadow over the once-quiet town. The decision to move the body marked a pivotal moment in the investigation, setting the stage for the official inquiry that would seek to unravel the mystery surrounding the untimely demise of Marcus Lyon.

As the community grappled with the shocking discovery of Marcus Lyon's lifeless body, a somber gathering convened at Sykes Tavern on Monday morning. A jury was assembled, and under the watchful eyes of those seeking answers, the body underwent a thorough examination by Dr. Samuel F. Merrick. With the utmost care, the remains were decently laid out, each detail scrutinized in the pursuit of justice.

The gathered evidence painted a harrowing picture: two large wounds marred the forehead, and the back of the head bore the brutal signs of bruising and a horrifying breakage. In a macabre revelation, it was uncovered that Marcus Lyon had also been shot in the right side. The bullet, prevented by a rib from penetrating deeply, was found lodged in the victim's clothing. The extent of the injuries pointed to a brutal and deliberate act of violence.

The solemn jury, after careful consideration, unanimously agreed on a verdict that echoed the gravity of the circumstances: willful murder. The haunting details of the autopsy painted a vivid portrait of the brutality inflicted on the unfortunate young man. It was surmised that the rapid and vicious nature of the attack left little room for a prolonged struggle for life, as evidenced by the lack of further signs of violence. The waters had quickly become the silent witness to Marcus Lyon's tragic demise, shrouding the last moments of his struggle beneath a cloak of darkness. The community now stood united in the pursuit of justice, seeking to bring those responsible for this heinous act to account.

In the wake of the grim discovery and the chilling verdict, swift action was taken to bring the perpetrators to justice. A messenger was dispatched to Springfield with urgency, carrying the weight of a community's resolve.

Marcus Lyon was found to be a native of Woodstock, Connecticut, and another messenger was dispatched with the mournful news to his family and friends. Marcus Lyon was unmarried and had a mother, sister and brother, all living in Woodstock. Marcus had been absent from his friends and family through the summer to work at Cazenovia and was from November 4 returning home. It was concluded that he had but a small sum of money with him, which the "greedy ruffians" took possession of.

On Tuesday, the mortal remains of Mr. Marcus Lyon were solemnly transported to his hometown in Woodstock. The funeral ceremony, a poignant display of Christian burial rites, drew an exceptionally large gathering. The community's outpouring of support and attendance was unprecedented, showcasing the deep respect and sorrow felt by those who gathered to bid farewell to their departed friend.

The final resting place of Marcus Lyon is now marked at Bungay Cemetery, located in the serene surroundings of West Woodstock, Connecticut. The tranquil setting of his burial site serves as a lasting tribute to his memory.

On Wednesday, during an examination of the presumed crime scene, a discerning individual observed a noteworthy discovery. Nestled in the bushes at a short distance, a second pistol was found, mirroring the positioning of the initial one. Evidently, this newly found firearm seemed to be a counterpart or mate to the first, adding a layer of intrigue to the circumstances.

As the wheels of justice began to turn, witnesses came forward with crucial information. Reports indicated that two men dressed as sailors were observed leaving Wilbraham in haste. The pursuit of the murderers took on a relentless pace, with authorities and concerned citizens determined to unravel the mystery surrounding Marcus Lyon's untimely demise. The echoes of this grim event reverberated through the region, and the pursuit of justice became a collective endeavor, driven by the shared goal of bringing closure to a haunted community.

The individuals under pursuit were traced back to Boston, and subsequently, they embarked on a journey toward New York. Their overnight stay on November 8 was in Western (Warren, Massachusetts). The following morning, they reached a store in Palmer near the meeting house, where they consumed spirits from a canister. About two miles from there, in the direction of Wilbraham, they emerged from a wooded area brandishing bludgeons, suggesting that they had recently acquired these weapons.

Continuing on their journey, the men stopped at a tavern about three miles east of the tragic spot to refresh themselves. Their actions were observed by numerous onlookers as they progressed. Notably, in proximity to the eventual crime scene, they encountered a local gentleman, engaging in inquiries about the distance to Springfield, the nature of the road and other details. These interactions raised suspicions and added to the unfolding narrative of their movements.

The next sighting of the individuals was reported by Laertes Fuller. It is strongly suggested that they likely fired on him and subsequently bludgeoned him to death with the pistols, leaving his lifeless body in the water as previously described. Following this tragic incident, the first subsequent sighting of the perpetrators was once again reported by Laertes. Notably, the boy, accompanying the horse, encountered the individuals, and it is beyond doubt that they directed the horse into a lot belonging to John Bliss.

The boy, who unwittingly followed these "ruffians," could have been in imminent danger. The individual sitting on the wall, while the other rode up the mountain, might have intended to silence the witness. The boy's apparent lack of knowledge or suspicion likely played a crucial role in sparing his life. This detail adds a chilling layer to the unfolding events.

The individuals were observed within about half a mile west of the harrowing crime scene, moving with remarkable speed. Their rapid passage took them westward, past the Glover Blacksmith Shop, situated at 43 Maple Street, as it is known today. Thomas Glover and Jeremy Bliss were present at the blacksmith shop and witnessed the two men as they hurriedly passed by.

The suspects were spotted at various locations along the road to Springfield, displaying a sense of urgency in their travel. Upon entering the town of Springfield, they were notably in a state of high perspiration, indicating the intensity and haste of their journey. Their trajectory led them toward the lower ferry, and there was a noticeable uneasiness in their efforts to expedite their passage.

Interestingly, the individuals were accompanied by a gentleman who crossed the Connecticut River with them, proceeding some distance toward Suffield, Connecticut. The suspects reached a tavern in the upper part of Suffield, Connecticut, early in the evening, seeking a brief respite and refreshment. Swiftly, they resumed their journey, making their way to Pickett's Tavern in Windsor, Connecticut, where they sought accommodations. Notably, their behavior drew attention. While waiting for supper, they were observed spending time away from the light, occasionally in a dark room or walking out the door.

Their actions at Pickett's Tavern raised suspicions, and as their supper was being prepared, they engaged in behavior that was deemed unusual. Despite settling in for the night with the intention of an early start the next morning, the circumstances surrounding their stay added an air of intrigue to their journey.

On Sunday, the suspects were in Hartford, Connecticut, where they efficiently took breakfast and hastened on their journey. Witnesses observed them traveling with notable speed along the road. By Tuesday morning, they had reached Greenwich, Connecticut, and were situated at Cos Cob Harbor, a mere thirty miles from New York by water, where they intended to sail shortly.

During their time at Cos Cob Harbor, the pursuers, Deputy Sheriff Josiah Bardwell of Springfield and Jeremy Bliss of Wilbraham, the same individual who had earlier witnessed the suspects passing the blacksmith shop with great haste, caught up to them. The pursuers arrived to apprehend both men for the alleged murder.

Interestingly, it seems that the suspects were unaware of being pursued until their apprehension. Upon being taken into custody, they reportedly offered no resistance. Instead, they professed their innocence and expressed a willingness to be searched and brought back to Massachusetts for trial.

In their possession, the suspects were found to have the aforementioned canister, a small quantity of cut shot and slightly less than twenty-two dollars in cash, along with a few articles of little value. Notably, their greatcoats revealed an intriguing detail—on the inner side of each coat, there was a pocket specifically designed for carrying pistols similar to the ones discovered near the tragic scene where Mr. Lyon's body was found. This discovery raised questions about the connection between the suspects and the crime they were accused of committing.

The suspects were identified as Dominic Daly, aged thirty-four, and James Halligan, aged twenty-seven, both of Irish descent and foreign birth. Halligan had originally resided in Hartford and was known for his good reputation in the community. On the other hand, Daly, the older of the two, projected a subtle demeanor. He had been in the country for a short duration and had family members, including a wife, in the eastern part of Massachusetts.

The suspects had departed from Boston a week before their apprehension and followed the main road leading from Boston to the point where they were ultimately arrested. The suspects, Dominic Daly and James Halligan, took five days from Tuesday to Saturday to cover the distance of about 80 miles from Boston to Wilbraham. This translates to a rate of travel of less than 20 miles per day during that initial stretch. However, the pace of their journey significantly accelerated from the afternoon of Saturday to the forenoon of Tuesday, covering the distance from Wilbraham to Greenwich, which is nearly 130 miles. This increased the rate of their journey to nearly 50 miles per day during this later period. The notable difference in their travel speeds raises natural suspicions and suggests that the change in pace might have been influenced by guilt and fear.

Following their apprehension, Dominic Daly and James Halligan were brought back to Springfield. Subsequently, on a Friday, witnesses were examined in the town house of Springfield, while the prisoners were ordered to be committed for trial before a court with appropriate jurisdiction. After this decision, they were transported to Northampton, which served as the seat of Hampshire County, where Wilbraham was located at that time. The legal proceedings and transfer to Northampton marked the next steps in the judicial process as they awaited trial for the charges against them.

On April 24, 1806, in the morning, the significant trial began in the meeting house in Northampton. The venue, however, proved insufficient to accommodate the large crowd that had gathered. The Honorable Judges Sedgwick and Sewall presided over the court, along with other individuals deemed suitable for the proceedings.

During the trial, witnesses were again examined, and the substance of their testimony was systematically arranged as follows:

1. Marcus Lyon left Cazenovia in the state of New York on November 4, 1805, in good health for his native place in Woodstock, Connecticut.
2. Marcus Lyon died on November 9 in Wilbraham.
3. Marcus Lyon was murdered through violence inflicted on him by a pair of horse pistols, and his body was disposed of in the Chicopee River, where it was later found.
4. Dominic Daly and James Halligan were traveling on the day of Lyon's death and naturally encountered him at the time and place of his fatal incident.
5. Dominic Daly, along with an associate, was discovered near the body of the deceased, alongside the well-known horse of Marcus Lyon, seemingly at the very hour of his death.

This systematic arrangement of testimony presented a compelling case against Dominic Daly and James Halligan, linking them directly to the circumstances surrounding Marcus Lyon's untimely demise.

During the trial, there was a lack of evidence presented by the defense to counteract the testimony provided by the prosecution. The government's case was supported by a strong narrative, and witnesses seemed to align with the prosecution's version of events.

Despite the absence of evidence to contradict the government's testimony, the defense, led by attorney F. Blake of Worcester, made an extensive, learned and eloquent plea on behalf of Dominic Daly and James Halligan. In their defense, it was acknowledged that Marcus Lyon had indeed been murdered, but the defense contended that the murder did not occur on November 9. Additionally, it was conceded that Daly and Halligan had traveled as the evidence indicated, but the defense argued that the timeline presented by the prosecution made it nearly impossible for the defendants to have committed the murder in the brief window of time described.

Specifically, the defense challenged the feasibility of the prisoners walking about 220 yards and completing the murder within the alleged fifteen-minute timeframe, as suggested by the testimony of the boy, L. Fuller. While it was not denied that, if the boy's evidence was considered valid, the defendants would likely be condemned, efforts were made to invalidate the boy's testimony. The defense questioned the reliability of the boy's identification of Daly based solely on facial features, suggesting that it was improbable for him to accurately recognize the prisoner in this manner. The defense's argument thus focused on raising doubts about the timeline and the boy's identification of the defendants.

The defense invested considerable effort in creating reasonable doubts in the minds of the jury, particularly concerning the testimony of the young witness. The defense multiplied its arguments to undermine the circumstances supporting the witness's testimony and to diminish its validity. Throughout the proceedings, every possible point that could be argued from the nature of things was brought forward, and the defense, benefiting from able lawyers, received keen attention in presenting its case.

The concluding plea was made by the attorney general, addressing and countering the arguments raised by the defense. The attorney general emphasized that, based on the evidence presented on behalf of the government, Marcus Lyon was murdered on November 9, 1805, in Wilbraham, as previously described. The assertion that the prisoners at the bar were the murderers was supported by the testimony of L. Fuller, along with numerous other consistent and corroborating circumstances.

The attorney general proceeded to highlight the inherent level of presumption in all evidence, noting that even the most positive testimony requires the presumption that the witness is testifying truthfully—an assumption that no jury can definitively ascertain. However, he argued that a certain level of uncertainty or doubt is not unreasonable and can be accepted. Moreover, he asserted that the doubts in this case did not surpass the doubts that naturally arise in the clearest evidence. Therefore, he concluded that the testimony presented was sufficient for conviction.

The prosecution presented its plea with forcefulness, directness and clarity, leaving the case in the clearest point of view. The honorable judges, in their charge to the jury, took them through the necessary points for consideration, guiding them to a clear understanding of their challenging duty.

The case was then submitted to the jury by the court, and the court adjourned between the hours of ten and eleven o'clock in the evening. Upon the jury's swift agreement, they delivered their verdict: guilty. The scene that unfolded in the courtroom was genuinely distressing, as the wife, mother and brother of Dominic Daly, who were present, were overwhelmed with grief and anguish in response to the verdict. The weight of the conviction brought forth a somber and emotional atmosphere in the courtroom.

The attorney general, representing the commonwealth, moved for the pronouncement of the death sentence against Dominic Daly and James Halligan. The Honorable Sedgwick, the presiding justice, then rose and conveyed the gravity of their crime in a solemn, impressive and affecting manner. He addressed the two defendants, saying, "You, Dominic Daly and James Halligan, have been favored with Counsel of your own choice, and a full jury of your own challenging, and are awarded guilty! Therefore, I have the painful task of informing you that for the murder of Marcus Lyon, according to the laws of our land, you must *die*."

The judge continued, stating that the two were to be remanded back to prison, where they would remain until the appointed time. On that day, they would be conducted to the place of execution, where they would be hanged by the neck until dead, and afterward their bodies would be subjected to anatomization. The severe and final nature of the pronouncement marked the culmination of the trial and set the course for the legal consequences of their actions.

Following are the last dying words of Dominic Daly and James Halligan, as pronounced by Daly at the gallows on June 5, 1806, and delivered in writing to General Mattoon:

> *At this awful moment of appearing before the tribunal of the almighty and knowing that telling a falsehood would be eternal perdition to our poor souls, We solemnly declare we are perfectly Innocent of the Crime for which we suffer, or any other Murder or Robbery; never saw, to our knowledge, Marcus Lyon in our lives; and as unaccountable as it may appear, the boy never saw one of us, looking at him, at, or near, a fence; or any of us either leading, driving, or riding a Horse; and we never went off the high road.*
>
> *We blame no one; we forgive everyone; we submit to our fate as being the will of the almighty; and beg him to be merciful to us, through the merits of his divine Son, our blessed Savior Jesus Christ. Our sincere thanks to the Rev. John Cheverus for his long and kind attention to us, as likewise every other friend that served us and comforted us during our long confinement.*

In the year 1806, Northampton, with a population of approximately 2,500 residents, became the site of a significant event drawing an unexpectedly large crowd. On June 5, 1806, around 15,000 people gathered at the Gallows Plains, marking the old main entrance to the Northampton State Hospital, to witness the execution of Dominic Daly and James Halligan. The substantial turnout reflected the morbid curiosity and heightened interest surrounding such somber and grave events.

Providing solace to the condemned men before their execution was Father Jean-Louis Lefebvre de Cheverus, who had been contacted by Daly upon receiving the death sentence for Marcus Lyon's murder. Father Cheverus

The gallows in Northampton, 1806. *Drawing by David Bourbeau.*

conducted their last rites in the Old Church, with an attentive crowd listening outside. The priest also delivered a sermon before the execution, marking a significant moment as the first Catholic mass in the area.

During his sermon, Father Cheverus addressed the troubling nature of the large audience, particularly admonishing women who appeared to attend out of morbid curiosity. He expressed disapproval for those finding pleasure in the suffering of others, deeming it a dishonor to virtue.

The challenges faced by Father Cheverus, such as having to stay at the jail before finding lodging, hint at an underlying anti-Catholic sentiment in the area. This aspect underscores the complex social dynamics and biases that prevailed during that historical period.

The bodies of Dominic Daly and James Halligan, following their execution, underwent autopsy at the Dickinson house on Maple Street. Subsequently, the remains went through the gruesome procedure of having the flesh boiled off the bones, a horrifying process that took place in the slaughterhouse near the South Street Bridge. These practices were often part of anatomical studies and dissections during that era, reflecting the macabre approaches to postmortem examinations and the study of human anatomy.

In 1836, an undocumented account suggests that the real killer of Marcus Lyon confessed on his deathbed, adding a layer of complexity and potential injustice to the historical narrative. The reported confession from the uncle of Laertes Fuller, the key witness in the prosecution's case, raises questions about the accuracy of the original trial and the guilt of Dominic Daly and James Halligan.

The absence of any mention of an appeal or judicial review of the death sentence for Daly and Halligan is notable and underscores the limitations and potential biases in the legal processes of that era. The historical context of the time, marked by social changes and the influx of new immigrants, particularly non-Protestant Irish, sheds light on the challenges and prejudices faced by these communities.

The portrayal of these Irish immigrants as poor, uneducated and Catholic reveals the discriminatory attitudes prevailing at the time. The fear, suspicion and hatred toward these newcomers likely influenced perceptions and may have played a role in the outcome of cases, such as the one involving Daly and Halligan. The observation that all evidence was circumstantial, with no solid proof or witnesses to the actual crime, emphasizes the potential flaws in the legal proceedings and the risks associated with biases against marginalized communities.

The exoneration of Dominic Daly and James Halligan on St. Patrick's Day in 1984 by Governor Michael Dukakis of Massachusetts represents a significant acknowledgment of potential injustice and a symbolic rectification of historical wrongs. Proclaiming to clear their names underscores a recognition that the legal proceedings in their case may have been flawed, and the exoneration seeks to set the record straight.

Governor Dukakis's proclamation taking place on St. Patrick's Day adds a poignant layer to the gesture. This act of exoneration serves as a posthumous acknowledgment of the wrongful conviction of Daly and Halligan, providing some measure of justice and closure for their memory and the broader historical narrative surrounding their case.

The enduring presence of two structures in Wilbraham that played a role in the historic murder trial adds a tangible connection to the past. The first, a stone bridge constructed in 1732 during the rerouting of the Bay Path, remains intact under the driveway of 2957 Boston Road. A hat, supposedly belonging to Marcus Lyon, was afterward found under this stone bridge that crossed over a small stream. This bridge, a witness to the changing landscape of the area, can be viewed best from the east side.

The second structure, an old blacksmith shop, stands in front of 51 Mountain Road. Initially built around 1795, it was originally located at 43 Maple Street, opposite Sykes Tavern, and played a role in the evidence presented during the 1805 murder trial. Operated by Thomas Glover, the blacksmith shop witnessed various relocations over the years. Around 1868, it moved to 19 Maple Street under the management of E.M. Barry until 1871. The final relocation occurred around 1877, placing it at 51 Mountain Road, where it stands today. These structures, with their rich history, serve as physical reminders of the events that unfolded in the past and their enduring impact on the local community.

THE HAUNTING SHADOWS OF DESOLATION

UNVEILING TRAGEDIES AT THE COLLINS PAPER MILL

In the dimly lit mill, workers toiled tirelessly amid cramped work areas, their movements restricted by the imposing presence of heavy machinery. The air hung thick with the acrid scent of dust and the constant hum of industrial activity. It was a scene of relentless labor, where the very conditions of their work posed myriad challenges and risks.

Within the narrow confines of the workplace, discomfort was a constant companion. The lack of space not only made the work arduous but also heightened the risk of accidents. The rhythmic pounding of machinery echoed through the air, drowning out any semblance of peace and quiet. Prolonged exposure to these thunderous sounds exacted a toll on the workers' hearing, a silent sacrifice to the relentless demands of industry.

Ventilation was a luxury the workers could ill afford. The stagnant air trapped within the confines of the mill carried a toxic cocktail of dust, fumes and pollutants. The workers breathed in this noxious air, their respiratory systems bearing the burden of an environment devoid of fresh, clean oxygen. The consequences were dire, with respiratory problems becoming an ever-present specter haunting the lives of those who toiled within.

As the machinery roared and the air thickened, the temperature swung from one extreme to another. The chill of cold metal surfaces in winter contrasted with the sweltering heat of molten industry in summer. Workers faced the relentless assault of these environmental extremes without proper protective measures, succumbing to illnesses, discomfort and a gradual erosion of vitality.

The machinery, with its gears and cogs, held the promise of progress but also carried the inherent danger of trauma. Workers risked life and limb, navigating a hazardous landscape where the slightest misstep could result in injury and even death. The toll of accidents and traumatic incidents soared, creating a pervasive sense of vulnerability among those who labored in the shadows of industrial giants.

Toxic exposures became an inescapable reality for these workers. Heavy metals dust, and solvents pervaded the air, seeping into the very fabric of their existence. The consequences were both acute and insidious—respiratory issues clawed at their lungs, and the slow poisoning cast a long shadow over their health.

In this harsh milieu, the phrase "mill fever" took on a sinister resonance. It wasn't merely an ailment—it was a dreaded affliction that claimed lives. The constant exposure to pollution and dust manifested in a range of respiratory and health problems, turning the air they breathed into a silent executioner.

The mortality rates painted a grim picture, revealing the heavy toll exacted by the combination of workplace hazards and inadequate healthcare. Workers, mere cogs in the industrial machinery, paid the ultimate price for progress.

Yet amid the harshness and adversity, a spark of resilience flickered. The plight of these workers became a rallying cry for change. Slowly but surely, the echoes of their struggles reverberated beyond the mill walls.

Collins Mill in the 1890s. *Atheneum Society of Wilbraham.*

Labor movements gained momentum, advocacy for workers' rights grew louder and a call for regulatory reforms became a beacon of hope. Over time, this collective outcry paved the way for the development of labor laws and regulations, marking a crucial step toward ensuring safer and healthier workplaces for future generations.

Within the walls and outside areas of the Collins Paper Mill, where the rhythmic hum of industry met the diligent efforts of its workers, there unfolded a series of tragedies that etched a somber narrative into the annals of its history. These stories, poignant and harrowing, bear witness to the harsh realities faced by those who toiled within its confines.

A tragic incident on Saturday night, March 9, 1889, cast a somber shadow over the history of the North Wilbraham paper mill, revealing the grim reality of the dangers that lurked within its walls. Patrick Carney, a dedicated employee, met a horrific fate that night, a victim of a workplace accident that would leave a lasting mark on the mill's grisly past.

Carney's responsibilities at the paper mill involved tending to the great vats where paper trimmings were boiled to create stock. On that ill-fated night, as he stood on the edge of the half-covered tank, diligently poking and stirring the boiling mixture of water and pulp, tragedy struck. The stick he used for his task abruptly broke, causing him to lose his balance and fall into the scalding tank.

His desperate attempt to cling to the tank's cover proved futile, and it was only through the swift action of his two companions, Fogerty and Dennis Powers, that Carney was rescued. However, the damage had been done. His body bore the brunt of the boiling water, and the skin peeled off in patches when his clothing was removed. The severity of his injuries was apparent, and the immediate response of Dr. Hannum of Ludlow and Holbrook of Palmer was sought.

Despite their efforts, Carney's condition continued to worsen. The scalding from the boiling water proved fatal, and he succumbed to his injuries on Sunday night around 8:00 p.m. Patrick Carney, about fifty years old, left behind a grieving widow and three sons. His eldest, Thomas, aged twenty-three, had once been a pitcher for the Springfield Nine, adding a poignant layer to the family's tragedy. The youngest son, just thirteen years old, faced the loss of his father at a tender age.

Another tragic incident involved William Dempsey on January 9, 1891. Dempsey, engaged in the demanding task of operating a duster machine alongside a fellow worker, found himself caught in a sequence of events that would lead to a horrific and fatal outcome.

As the duster machine diligently performed its function, it became overloaded with rags. The strain on the machine caused the belt to slip off the pulley above, prompting Mr. Dempsey and his colleague to intervene. In a bid to rectify the situation, Dempsey attempted to put the belt back onto the pulley. However, this seemingly routine task took a tragic turn as the belt became entangled in the surrounding machinery.

The machinery's relentless pull drew the belt into a perilous dance with the shafting, counter shafting, hangers and pulleys, creating a cascade of mechanical chaos. In the midst of this unfortunate series of events, one of the hangers dislodged and fell, striking Mr. Dempsey to the floor with a fatal force.

As he lay on the floor, the full weight of the mechanism above descended on him, a crushing force that left him with a grievously injured head and both legs broken. The severity of his injuries became apparent, and despite any medical intervention, William Dempsey succumbed to his wounds about thirty-six hours later.

On Sunday afternoon, November 4, 1894, another somber chapter in the history of the paper mill claimed the life of John Shepard, a fifty-three-year-old carpenter dedicated to his work. Engaged in a routine task, Shepard's life was cut short in a heartbreaking manner.

Around 3:00 p.m., John Shepard was undertaking the responsibility of putting a belt onto one of the large wheels within the mill. However, in a devastating turn of events, the wheel was set in motion while he was still engaged in the task. Caught off guard, Shepard slipped and was swiftly entangled in the relentless gears of the machinery.

As he was dragged through the unforgiving gear system, the force proved fatal. The accident resulted in the breaking of his neck, causing instantaneous and tragic death. The mill's machinery, which had once been the heartbeat of industry, became an unwitting instrument in the untimely demise of a dedicated worker. John Shepard's passing left a profound impact on those who knew him, and it reverberated beyond the industrial confines. He was survived by a grieving widow and three children—two boys and a girl.

Tragedy struck millworkers as well as anyone who lived or played nearby. The unusual death of Maurice Murphy on January 15, 1903, paints a heart-wrenching picture of a young life cut short in a seemingly innocent moment of joy. Maurice, the eight-year-old son of P.J. Murphy, met a strange fate at the paper mill, casting a somber pall over the community.

Around 4:00 p.m., Maurice was joyfully sliding down a sharp hill that began at the freight house, a structure that still stands today. The course extended for 520 feet, culminating on a footbridge that spanned across the canal to the mill. In the midst of this childhood pastime, tragedy struck.

As Maurice slid down the hill on his sled, he lost control of the makeshift vehicle. The sled careened off course, striking the side rail of the footbridge. In a cruel twist of fate, Maurice was thrown into the open water of the canal, where the current swiftly carried him beneath the ice-covered surface.

Upon realizing the gravity of the situation, the paper mill was immediately shut down, and efforts were made to draw water from the canal in a desperate attempt to reach the young boy. Despite the swift response and every effort to revive him, Maurice stayed submerged in the icy water for about thirty minutes, rendering the attempts to restore him futile.

The tragic incident left Maurice's family in mourning. He was survived by his parents, a sister and a brother named Thomas, each grappling with the profound loss of a beloved son and sibling. The circumstances surrounding Maurice's death serve as a poignant reminder of the unexpected and unpredictable nature of life, even in the midst of seemingly innocent childhood activities.

Another tragic event that happened to the same Murphy family unfolded on December 22, 1910, with the subsequent passing of Thomas P. Murphy. Thomas, a twenty-one-year-old machinist employed at the Cutler mill, located near the paper mill, became a victim of a horrific workplace accident that would ultimately claim his life.

On that fateful day, while diligently working on the machinery, Thomas found himself entangled in the very gears and mechanisms he sought to maintain. The machinery proved unforgiving, and Thomas suffered the devastating loss of his left leg, an injury that would prove fatal in the days to come.

In the immediate aftermath of the accident, Thomas was attended to by Dr. Calkins, who provided medical care and oversaw his transportation to Mercy Hospital in Springfield. Despite the efforts to save him, Thomas succumbed to "blood poisoning" on January 2, 1911, marking the end of a young life filled with promise. The proximity of these two tragic incidents, both in terms of location and familial relation, cast a shadow over the town of Wilbraham.

The untimely death of James Fitzgerald on the morning of January 20, 1906, at the Collins Manufacturing Company's boardinghouse cast another shadow over the community. At twenty-eight years old, James was found lifeless in bed, a sudden and unexpected loss that left those who knew him in shock.

The preceding night had been seemingly unremarkable, with James working and appearing to be in good spirits and health. However, the following morning, his absence at the breakfast table raised concerns. Mrs. E. Cronin, his boarding mistress, took notice and, suspecting that he might not be feeling well, decided to bring his breakfast to his room.

Upon reaching James's door around 7:15 a.m., Mrs. Cronin's attempts to elicit a response went unanswered. Fearing the worst, she sought to enter the room and discovered that the door, bolted from the inside, required intervention. Upon gaining access, a somber discovery awaited her: James Fitzgerald lay lifeless in his bed.

Dr. A.L. Damon was promptly summoned, and he, in turn, reached out to Medical Examiner Bates of Springfield. The official cause of death was pronounced as an acute congestion of the lungs, a sudden and severe condition that had claimed James's life in the quiet of the night. In the aftermath, James's body was taken to the home of his aunt, Mrs. Mary, where grieving friends and family gathered to mourn his passing.

The incident involving James Powers on the afternoon of August 13, 1906, highlights the risks and injuries that industrial workers faced during this period. James, employed at the paper mill, suffered a serious injury when his foot was badly crushed in an accident involving the freight elevator within the mill premises. As James rode in the freight elevator, with one foot positioned against the side of the elevator, it became ensnared, resulting in a severe crushing injury. The nature of the accident prompted the immediate need for medical attention.

Dr. A.L. Damon was called to the scene to provide initial medical care and dressing for the injured foot. Recognizing the potential severity of the injury, Dr. Damon ordered James Powers to be transferred to Mercy Hospital in the city of Springfield for further evaluation.

The decision was made to have an X-ray done at the hospital to assess the extent of the damage. X-rays would have provided crucial insights into the internal injuries, aiding medical professionals in devising an appropriate course of treatment for James's recovery. The swift response by Dr. Damon and the decision to seek specialized medical care at Mercy Hospital underscores the importance of timely and thorough medical evaluation in cases of workplace injuries.

The unfortunate incident involving Ureo Brackiniski on January 15, 1913, serves as a cautionary tale about the dangers of curiosity and the unexpected hazards that could be present in industrial settings. While diligently working in the rag room at the paper mill, Ureo stumbled upon an object within the rags. Intrigued and unaware of its nature, curiosity got the better of him, prompting him to attempt opening it with his knife. Little did he know that this seemingly innocent act would have dire consequences.

The decision to pry open the unknown object resulted in an explosion that inflicted serious injuries. The blast blew off the first joint of his thumb and the first two joints of his index finger on his right hand. Following the incident, Ureo received crucial first-aid treatment, highlighting the importance of swift response and medical care in such emergencies. He was then transported to Springfield Hospital for further assessment and treatment. Upon examination, it was determined that the object Ureo had been attempting to open with his knife was, in fact, a dynamite cartridge.

On April 2, 1913, Gus Cameron, a paper hanger stationed in the loft of the paper mill, endured a painful accident while performing his duties. As he pulled a load of paper into the machine room, a large machine knife dislodged during the operation and struck Gus's hand as it fell. The impact of the falling knife resulted in a gash three inches long in the back of his left hand. The laceration necessitated immediate medical attention and intervention. To close the deep wound, Gus Cameron required eight stitches.

Brian Fallon, a dedicated employee with twenty-three years of service at the mill, met a fatal end while carrying out his duties. On that fateful day, he was engaged in putting up storm windows within the mill. However, a slip led to a devastating fall into one of the machines, where he became entangled in the gears, resulting in severe injuries. Despite his years of experience and dedication to the mill, this unfortunate accident claimed his life. Brian had transitioned to the role of a watchman in recent times, emphasizing the unpredictable nature of workplace accidents.

A postcard of the Collins Manufacturing Company, early 1900s. *Atheneum Society of Wilbraham.*

He left behind three daughters and three sons, all residing in North Wilbraham. The impact of his loss would undoubtedly have been profound on his family and the community. The mourning process and arrangements were initiated promptly, with the body taken to Holyoke for the funeral, which was held at the Dillon Undertaker Rooms the next morning. Brian Fallon found his final resting place in Palmer at St. Thomas Cemetery.

Do you believe in ghosts? This old paper mill is believed to be haunted. An incident that happened around 2010 was relayed to me by the property manager of the mill a few years ago. One day, Doug was tending the boilers in the old boiler room when he turned around and saw a full apparition of his old boss, Max, who owned the mill before his death two years before. Max never liked Doug being in the boiler room for some unknown reason, so he believes that Max was checking on him. Doug also stated that he would hear footsteps and the creaking of the floorboards of the floors above when he knew no one else was in the building. During the many times I have visited this mill, I have always felt a sense of uneasiness that I just could not explain.

As I ponder the stories whispered within the aging walls of the mill, I can't help but wonder. Are we truly alone in this world, or are there forces beyond our comprehension, lingering just beyond the veil of perception? The old paper mill stands as a silent sentinel to such questions, its halls echoing with the whispers of the past and the mysteries of the unknown.

ABEL'S PRETENTIOUS NEW HOME

Abel Bliss, born on February 18, 1708, in Springfield, Massachusetts, was a man of both physical strength and determination. On January 16, 1736, he married Jemima Chapin, a woman with deep roots in the region. Jemima, born on January 5, 1705, in Springfield (now Chicopee), Massachusetts, was the daughter of John Chapin and Sarah Bridgman and the great-granddaughter of the esteemed Deacon Samuel Chapin, an early immigrant of Springfield, Massachusetts.

After their union, Abel and Jemima set their sights on forging a new life together. The couple became pioneers, leaving Abel's hometown of Springfield to embrace the challenges and opportunities of the Outward Commons (Wilbraham). Their journey in 1736 marked the beginning of a legacy that would contribute significantly to the early development of this town.

Upon arriving in the Outward Commons, the couple faced the daunting task of establishing a homestead. Abel, known for his physical prowess, took charge of constructing their first home in the mountains, a log cabin near 223 Mountain Road. However, the chosen location presented practical challenges—it was not close to any spring or brook, making access to water a daily struggle. During those times, digging wells was not a common practice, adding another layer of complexity to their living situation.

Abel's reputation for strength was put to the test as he, alongside fellow settler Thomas Merrick, worked tirelessly to cut another path from Springfield to Wilbraham, a vital link that would connect the burgeoning community to the outside world.

Amid these challenges, Abel and Jemima became the proud parents of five children, raising them against the backdrop of the evolving landscape of the Outward Commons. Abel's involvement in drawing up a petition around 1740 to establish the Outward Commons as a separate precinct showcased his commitment to the community's growth.

The Bliss cabin, despite its initial impracticality, became a symbol of resilience and determination. The couple's journey encapsulated the essence of early colonial life, marked by hardships and triumphs. Abel Bliss and Jemima Chapin's story remains woven into the fabric of Wilbraham's history, a testament to the spirit of those who shaped the foundations of the growing town.

Abel Bliss not only played a pivotal role in the early development of the Outward Commons but also answered the call to serve his community and country. Commissioned as an officer in the military sometime before 1754, Abel embarked on a journey that would add a new chapter to his story.

Before the outbreak of the French and Indian War, Abel Bliss, then around forty-five years old, found himself on the training field in July 1754, mustered with the South Hampshire (Massachusetts) Regiment. His military service took a significant turn when he received an ensign's commission under Colonel Worthington of Springfield, a recognition of his leadership and commitment to the cause. This commission, dated August 27, 1754, marked Abel's commitment within the ranks of the military.

Abel Bliss, now an ensign, might have seen action in the tumultuous times of the French and Indian War, a conflict that shaped the landscape of North America. His dedication to the military cause reflected the spirit of the times as tensions rose on the frontier.

Furthermore, Abel's commitment extended beyond the military realm. He received a justice's commission under the Crown from Governor William Shirley before 1759, showcasing his involvement in civic duties and the administration of justice within the growing community. Abel Bliss, once a pioneer settling in the Outward Commons, now became a multifaceted figure, contributing not only to the physical development of the town but also to its defense and governance.

The Bliss household, led by Abel and supported by Jemima, became a hub of resilience and service. Their story now intertwined with the broader historical narrative of colonial America, capturing the essence of a man who wore not only the hat of a settler but also the uniform of a military officer and the responsibilities of local justice.

Abel demonstrated his entrepreneurial spirit in raising the necessary funds for the construction of a new house; he set up a tar kiln along the river. This involved gathering candlewood from the surrounding area, likely a mixture of resinous and combustible materials suitable for the tar-making process.

Abel Bliss's tar kiln became a center of activity, where he applied his skills to produce tar as a byproduct of his candlewood operation. Remarkably, he succeeded in creating two hundred barrels of tar, a substantial quantity for the time. Abel then seized the opportunity to sell the tar, converting this byproduct into a valuable commodity that would help finance the construction of his house.

The construction of Abel Bliss's second home, a grand two-story house at 182 Mountain Road in 1744, marked a significant event in the history of the region. The house, boasting dimensions of thirty-two by forty feet, was considered the tallest ever built in the mountains up to that date, showcasing Abel's ambition and prosperity.

However, the tale takes an intriguing turn as Abel's plans clashed with the views of the formidable Worthy Noah Merrick, the pastor of the community. Upon learning about the ambitious project, Pastor Merrick, concerned about potential worldly pride among his parishioners, decided to address the matter promptly.

Abel Bliss home, circa 1913, looking southeast. *Joe Roberts.*

Abel Bliss home, circa 1913, looking northeast. *Joe Roberts.*

One Sunday morning, Pastor Merrick chose a sermon with a pointed message: "Build not your house too high." The direct reference to Abel's construction plans was clear, serving as a rebuke aimed at curbing any perceived arrogance or excess.

Responding with humility and penitence, Abel Bliss heeded the pastor's counsel. In a gesture of compliance, he took action to align with the sermon's message. Abel, with a sense of reverence for the spiritual guidance offered, decided to modify his grand design. The upright posts of the house, representing its height, were cut off by approximately seven feet. This alteration resulted in the first story being lowered accordingly.

The house, now modified to meet the pastor's admonition, became a symbol of both architectural prowess and humility. Interestingly, it is said that this house was the first in the region to feature square panes of glass in the windows. This departure from the traditional diamond-shaped panes set in lead reflected not only Abel's commitment to modernity but also his adaptability in the face of community expectations.

Abel Bliss's house, with its unique history of construction and adaptation, stands as a testament to the complex interplay between the material and spiritual aspects of life in early colonial America. The events surrounding the building of this house capture the dynamics of a community where religious guidance and societal expectations played a role in shaping even the physical landscape.

The historical context surrounding Abel Bliss's property at 182 Mountain Road in Wilbraham gains even more significance with the mention of the Bay Path, a crucial route during the plantation and colonial period.

The Bay Path, a significant road during the early years of settlement, served as a vital connection between Boston and Springfield, linking the eastern and western parts of the Massachusetts Bay Colony. This route played a pivotal role in facilitating trade, communication and the movement of settlers between the coastal areas and the interior.

Interestingly, the Bay Path originally passed along the back side of Abel Bliss's property, extending to Twelve Mile Brook and then following the course of Calkins Brook into Monson. This specific route was established around 1636 and remained in use until 1732. The path provided a direct link from Boston to Springfield and beyond, enabling the flow of people and goods through the region.

However, in 1732, a significant change occurred when this section of the Bay Path was discontinued. The road was rerouted slightly northward and connected to the present-day Boston just after going over the old stone bridge that crosses Spear Brook. Abel Bliss's property, situated in proximity to this historical route, would have witnessed the comings and goings of travelers and traders as they navigated the Bay Path.

The conclusion of Abel Bliss's life adds a poignant chapter to his story. Ensign Abel Bliss, a man of strength, resilience and multiple accomplishments, passed away on April 30, 1762.

Following Abel's passing, his wife, Jemima, continued to be a part of the community. She navigated life as a widow and, like her late husband, played a role in the development of the family and the community. Jemima Bliss lived until January 9, 1772, leaving behind a legacy intertwined with the growth and history of the Outward Commons, which became the town of Wilbraham in 1763.

Both Abel and Jemima found their final resting places at Adams Cemetery, where the stories of many early settlers are preserved. This burial ground became a place of remembrance for the Bliss family, as several of their children, grandchildren and beyond were later laid to rest alongside them.

The family plots serve as a tangible connection to the past, a place where the history of generations is etched into the landscape.

The insights provided by Antonette Catherine Mary Bliss (Speer) in her letter dated December 30, 1878, add fascinating details to the history of the Bliss family and their homestead:

Use of the Log Cabin as a Smallpox Hospital

The original log cabin in the "old orchard" served a unique and important purpose. It was utilized as a hospital during times when travelers or soldiers unfortunate enough to have contracted smallpox needed care.

Remnant of the Altered House Frame

Antonette stated that she found one of the upright timbers approximately seven feet in length that was cut by her great-grandfather from the frame of the new house under the house. This was in response to Reverend Noah Merrick's fierce sermon. It would be interesting to know if that piece of wood is still in existence.

Tavern and the Passing of General George Washington

The Bliss house served as a tavern at some point in its history. The Bay Path, which passed over the hill alongside their property, witnessed the passage of General George Washington to and from Boston. Antonette's recollection includes the image of her father, John Bliss, and other boys going out to the corner to witness Washington's passing, with the stately chieftain graciously acknowledging them with a bow.

Connection to Historical Events

The Bliss property played a role in historical events, including the aftermath of Marcus Lyon's murder. His saddled horse was discovered in Bliss's pasture the following day. The property and stone wall associated with this incident still existed during Antonette's time. Furthermore, John Bliss had to travel to Northampton as a witness in the Halligan and Daly trial related to the murder.

Soldiers Returning from the Revolutionary War

Antonette's recollections include stories of soldiers returning from the Revolutionary War. These soldiers spent the night at the Bliss house, stacking their guns in the corner and sleeping on the floor with their feet toward the fire.

THE BIRTHPLACE OF WILBRAHAM'S "ETHELBERT PEACHES"

Born in the quaint town of Monson on January 28, 1852, Ethelbert Bliss entered the world as the cherished child of Albert and Orpha Bishop Bliss. The Bliss family journeyed to Wilbraham in 1870, seeking new opportunities and a fresh start. Young Ethelbert eagerly embraced agricultural life, working alongside his father on the family farm.

In 1873, at the age of twenty-one, Ethelbert embarked on another significant journey—marriage to the love of his life, Abbie Cross. Their union blossomed, and by April 1875, the Bliss household echoed with the joyous cries of their first child, Walter Marshall Bliss. The family continued to grow with the arrival of Hattie Estella Bliss in August 1877 and Dora A. Bliss in March 1882.

The Bliss farm, a picturesque homestead with two charming homes, stood as a testament to generations past. The older house, at 1004 Main Street, had been built in 1761 by Thomas Mirick and his son Timothy. This dwelling became the cherished abode for Ethelbert and his growing family. Across the road, at 1003 Main Street, a newer house stood proudly, constructed in 1852 by Porter Cross on the historic site of Thomas Mirick's second homestead. Remarkably, this house remains standing today, a living relic of the Bliss family's enduring legacy.

The Bliss farm, though initially modest, thrived with a diverse range of agricultural pursuits, including the tender care of dairy cows. The landscape brimmed with the sounds of daily life, the bustling activities of a family deeply rooted in their land.

Ethelbert Bliss. *Wilbraham Public Library.*

Notably, Ethelbert's parents occupied the newer house across the road, maintaining a close-knit family bond. The Bliss family's connection to the land and one another became an enduring legacy of Wilbraham's history. As a side note, it's worth mentioning that this particular Bliss family shared no immediate ties with the Abel Bliss family, distinguished pioneers of Springfield Mountain (Wilbraham).

The Bliss family's homestead on Main Street near the Wilbraham/Hampden town line, known as Mapleside Farm, not only stands as a testament to their endeavors but also holds a unique place in local history. This picturesque locale earned its fame as the birthplace of the renowned Wilbraham peaches, a fact that contributed to its popularity in its heyday.

However, the roots of this land delve even deeper into the annals of time. Mapleside Farm was once part of the original farmstead of Lieutenant Thomas and Mary Merrick, pioneers who settled in the Outward Commons or Springfield Mountain in 1734, the early days of the settlement.

The farm gained historical notoriety in 1761 due to the tragic Timothy Merrick rattlesnake incident. This event, etched in the local lore, marked a significant chapter in the history of the land.

As Mapleside Farm continued to evolve through the Bliss family's stewardship, it retained its agricultural significance, becoming synonymous with the luscious Wilbraham peaches. The orchards, nurtured by the Bliss family's dedication to the land, bore fruit not only in harvest but also in the rich history that unfolded on this soil.

In revisiting the tale of Mapleside Farm, we unearth not only the Bliss family's contributions but also the enduring legacy of the Merrick family—a narrative that is deeply connected with the Outward Commons and Springfield Mountain. The echoes of their stories resonate through time, connecting the past to the present and imparting a sense of continuity to this cherished piece of local heritage.

The year 1876 marked a pivotal moment in the history of Mapleside Farm, as Albert Bliss and his son Ethelbert embarked on a daring experiment that would forever alter the landscape and reputation of their homestead.

Mapleside Farm, 1902. *Shelby Cubin.*

In a bold move, they planted one hundred peach trees on the farm they had acquired in 1870, signaling a shift in the farm's mission and laying the groundwork for Wilbraham's emergence as the peach center of the Connecticut River Valley.

The Bliss family's visionary decision bore its first fruits, quite literally, in the fourth year after the initial plantings. A bountiful crop of peaches flourished, adorning the orchards with vibrant colors and filling the air with the sweet fragrance of success. The success of this harvest marked a promising era for Mapleside Farm and cemented its growing reputation as a peach haven.

However, as with any agricultural venture, challenges loomed on the horizon. In the wake of the successful peach harvest, the Bliss family seeded the surrounding land with grass, reaping the rewards of an excellent crop. Yet despite their initial triumph, the peach trees, unfortunately, succumbed. The once-thriving orchards faced an unforeseen setback, leaving the Bliss family to grapple with the delicate balance of nature and agricultural pursuits.

The late nineteenth century brought both challenges and triumphs to Mapleside Farm, as the Bliss family's peach orchards faced a rollercoaster of success and setbacks. Around 1882, a neighboring farmer, William Sessions, embarked on a peach-growing venture, planting a substantial two hundred or more peach trees on his farm in Hampden, just half a mile south of Mapleside Farm. Mirroring the Bliss family's experience, Sessions enjoyed a profitable crop of peaches about four years later. However, history repeated itself as he, too, faced the disappointment of losing the trees after seeding the land with grass.

Undeterred by past setbacks, Ethelbert Bliss demonstrated an unyielding determination to realize his dream of flourishing peach orchards. In the spirit of continuous learning, he delved into the intricacies of peach cultivation, attending lectures and studying the art of nurturing these delicate fruits. In the spring of 1894, Ethelbert embarked on a bold venture, planting a staggering 1,400 new peach trees, predominantly of the Crosby variety.

The fruits of his labor were evident by the fall of 1897 when more than 1,000 baskets of high-quality peaches were harvested from Mapleside Farm. Ethelbert's dedication and expertise bore even greater results the following years, with 2,500 baskets in 1898 and a remarkable 4,500 baskets in the subsequent year. Ethelbert Bliss's commitment to the cultivation of peaches had transformed Mapleside Farm into a thriving orchard.

The success story of Mapleside Farm gained widespread recognition, and Ethelbert Bliss's dedication was featured in the October 1899 edition of the *Homestead*. By this time, the total number of peach trees under his care had reached an impressive five thousand, solidifying his status as a regional leader in peach production. Ethelbert Bliss had not only preserved but significantly expanded the legacy of Mapleside Farm, making it a beacon of success in the Connecticut River Valley.

Ethelbert Bliss's success in peach cultivation at Mapleside Farm was not just a stroke of luck; it was a result of strategic and innovative farming practices. One key factor contributing to his triumph was the continuous operation of a machine throughout the summer. This machine served the crucial purpose of spading around the roots of the peach trees, especially in areas where conventional cultivators faced challenges due to difficult soil conditions.

By running this machine tirelessly throughout the summer months, Ethelbert effectively addressed the unique soil conditions of his orchards. The spading process provided the necessary aeration and care for the roots, promoting optimal peach tree health and growth. This approach showcased Ethelbert's understanding of the specific needs of peach trees and his commitment to overcoming the challenges posed by the local terrain.

In a departure from traditional practices, Ethelbert made a deliberate choice not to sow grass seed in his peach orchards. This decision likely contributed to better resource allocation, allowing the peach trees to thrive without competition for nutrients from grass. The absence of grass seeding may have further streamlined the farming process, focusing resources on the peach trees and enhancing overall orchard productivity.

The birth of the commercial peach industry in Wilbraham, spearheaded by Ethelbert Bliss and Mapleside Farm, marked a significant milestone in the local agricultural landscape. However, as with any agricultural endeavor, challenges were inherent in the newfound industry.

The peach industry in Wilbraham faced numerous hurdles, primarily due to the vulnerabilities of peach trees. These challenges included natural adversaries such as animal and insect enemies that posed a threat to the health and productivity of the orchards. Protecting the delicate fruit buds became a constant battle against these forces of nature.

Additionally, the commercial peach industry grappled with the unpredictable and often harsh New England weather. The tender fruit buds were particularly susceptible to damage during occasional late spring heavy frosts, which could follow periods of warm weather. The vulnerability of the buds to frost presented a significant risk to the peach harvest, as frost could compromise the viability of the blossoms and, consequently, the yield of the orchards.

The delicate balance between tending to the needs of the peach trees, combating pests and navigating the whims of the weather underscored the complexity of the commercial peach industry in Wilbraham. Farmers like Ethelbert Bliss had to employ a combination of experience, innovation and resilience to sustain and expand their peach orchards.

Ethelbert Bliss's passion for peach cultivation wasn't limited to his own success; he actively sought to share his expertise with fellow farmers, aspiring to advance the field through collaborative efforts. His commitment to developing the "perfect peach" became a cornerstone of his reputation, and his willingness to experiment with new methods set him apart in the farming community.

Beyond his peach orchards, Ethelbert diversified Mapleside Farm's offerings, expanding into dairy farming. By 1899, the farm had become a hub for milk production, boasting a herd of twenty-five cows and heifers led by a registered Holstein bull. Ethelbert took a hands-on approach, closely monitoring his cattle and measuring their milk production. This meticulous care and attention contributed to the overall well-being of the herd and the quality of the milk they produced.

One of Ethelbert's distinctive practices was cultivating all the fodder required for the cattle on the farm itself. This approach showcased his commitment to self-sufficiency as well as emphasized the belief in the "value of silage for dairy cattle." Ethelbert's dedication to providing his cattle with high-quality feed contributed to their health and, in turn, enhanced milk production.

The results were impressive, with Mapleside Farm yielding more than ten thousand pounds of good milk in a single year. Ethelbert Bliss's integrated approach to agriculture, blending peach cultivation with dairy farming, highlighted his forward-thinking mindset. His commitment to sharing knowledge and embracing new developments in both fields left an indelible mark on the agricultural community, solidifying his legacy as a farmer who not only cultivated perfect peaches but also excelled in the art of dairy farming.

A testament to his lifelong dedication to peach culture was the remarkable achievement of developing the first strain of peaches specifically engineered to withstand the harsh winters of New England. Named after their creator, these resilient fruits became known as "Ethelbert Peaches." This groundbreaking accomplishment not only showcased Ethelbert's expertise but also marked a significant advancement in peach cultivation.

The introduction of Ethelbert Peaches signified a turning point in the local peach industry. These robust fruits, designed to endure the challenging climate of New England, represented a triumph of agricultural ingenuity. While the Ethelbert Peaches became renowned for their durability and adaptability, the continuous pursuit of improvement and the advent of newer and better peach varieties remained a hallmark of the ever-evolving agricultural landscape.

By the early twentieth century, Wilbraham had earned a prominent reputation as the premier destination for peaches. Ethelbert Bliss's contributions played a crucial role in establishing the town as a hub for innovative peach cultivation. The legacy of Ethelbert Peaches, though evolving with time, laid the foundation for ongoing advancements in peach varieties, reinforcing Wilbraham's standing as a leader in the peach industry.

At this same time, a significant expansion of the peach industry in Wilbraham occurred, spurred by the success of pioneering farmers like Ethelbert Bliss. Not long after 1900, Charles C. Beebe, Clarence P. Bolles and Jesse L. Rice took a bold step by establishing peach orchards at higher elevations than those of Ethelbert Bliss. The decision proved to be remarkably favorable, yielding more positive results for their peach cultivation endeavors.

By 1911, this trend had gained momentum, with several other farmers joining the ranks of peach growers in Wilbraham. D.H. Eaton, John J.

Lyons, M.C. Wade, W.H. McGuire, James Powers, Lee W. Rice and Herbert Merrick all embarked on setting up peach orchards as part of their farming ventures. The collaborative efforts of these farmers contributed to a notable increase in the scale of peach production in the region.

The year 1911 emerged as a particularly profitable one for Wilbraham peaches. The collective efforts of the growing number of peach orchards resulted in the sale of an impressive thirty to forty thousand baskets. This success underscored Wilbraham's burgeoning reputation as a key player in the peach market.

Among the farmers, Lee Rice emerged as a significant contributor, becoming the largest producer in town. His dedication to peach cultivation further solidified Wilbraham's standing, as the quantity of his peaches in the market continued to enhance the town's reputation for producing the finest peaches. The quality of Wilbraham peaches became a distinguishing feature. Described as having the "best color and finest flavor," the peaches from Wilbraham stood out in the markets.

The collaborative efforts of these farmers in Wilbraham not only expanded the peach industry but also elevated the town's status as a renowned hub for high-quality peaches, making a lasting impact on the agricultural legacy of the region.

The early days of peach marketing in Wilbraham were characterized by a combination of hard work, dedication and a reliance on horse-drawn wagons. Marketing peaches during this era was a labor-intensive process that required careful planning and an early start.

Farmers engaged in peach marketing would prepare specially built wagons loaded with prized fruits. These wagons, often hitched to horse teams, became the vessels for transporting the bountiful harvest to the Springfield commission markets. The journey commenced early in the morning, with some farmers leaving Wilbraham as early as two or three o'clock to ensure a timely arrival at the markets.

The sight of these peach-laden wagons drawn by four-horse teams would become a familiar one on the outskirts of Springfield. As the farmers approached the commission markets, a competitive spirit emerged among them. A line of ten to twelve wagons would form, each vying for the coveted first position in line. This negotiation process reflected the importance of securing a prime spot in the market, where the early bird often got the best opportunities for selling their peaches.

The dedication and effort invested in this early-morning journey underscored the commitment of Wilbraham's peach farmers to bring their produce to market promptly. The horse-drawn wagons were not only a means of transportation but also symbols of the hard work and entrepreneurial spirit that defined the early peach industry in the region.

This snapshot from the past provides a glimpse into the challenges and camaraderie among Wilbraham's peach farmers as they navigated the bustling commission markets of Springfield, marking a chapter in the history of the town's vibrant agricultural heritage.

Having transformed his father's farm into a thriving peach orchard, Ethelbert witnessed the continuity of his legacy through his son, Walter Marshall Bliss, who followed in his farming footsteps. The familial ties to the land deepened as his married daughters and their families established their homes and farms nearby, fostering a sense of community and shared agricultural heritage.

In 1950, the town of Wilbraham recognized Ethelbert Bliss as its oldest living citizen, a testament to his enduring presence and the impact he had on the local community. His life encapsulated the resilience and spirit of the early farmers who shaped Wilbraham's reputation as a prominent peach center.

As Ethelbert Bliss passed away in 1951 at the age of ninety-nine, the town mourned the loss of a man whose vision and hard work had bestowed on Wilbraham a fame in the arena of peach cultivation. Ethelbert Bliss deserves to be remembered not only as a peach pioneer but also as a steward of the land, a family man and a symbol of the agricultural vitality that shaped Wilbraham's identity. His legacy lives on in the orchards, the landscape and the collective memory of a town that he helped elevate to prominence in the world of peaches.

"YE OLDE" BURYING GROUND AND ITS SHADOWS AMONG THE TOMBSTONES

In the summer of 1730, the rugged and untamed "Mountains," coined the "Outward Commons," witnessed the arrival of the first settler, Nathaniel Hitchcock. Armed with determination, Hitchcock cleared two acres of land on the west side of the West Road (603 Main Street) and erected a modest log hut. However, it wasn't until the following spring, in May 1731, that he and his family decided to make this wild and beautiful place their permanent home.

As word of Hitchcock's venture spread, a trickle of intrepid families began to follow suit, gradually populating the area over the next few years. By January 1, 1741, this budding community boasted around twenty-six families and had welcomed thirty-eight newborns into the fold. The "Mountains" were beginning to transform from a solitary outpost into a vibrant settlement.

By May 1740, the community faced a significant challenge. The distance to Springfield for public worship at the "Old First" church, a daunting nine miles, posed a considerable hardship. The harsh winter conditions made the journey even more treacherous, especially as many families lacked horses and traversed the distance on foot. In response, the settlers rallied and drafted a petition to the General Court, seeking independence as a precinct and the right to build their own meeting house for communal worship.

Their plea found favor, and on January 6, 1741, the Outward Commons on the east side of the majestic Connecticut River officially became the

Fourth Precinct of Springfield. The newfound autonomy brought with it a sense of responsibility and excitement. Now the settlers faced the task of finding a minister and a suitable location for their meeting house.

On May 26, 1741, their prayers were answered when Mr. Noah Mirick (Merrick), a revered clergyman, accepted the call to minister among the people of the Mountains. Later on, the chosen spot for the meeting house was a picturesque stretch of land nestled between the Second and Third Divisions, known colloquially as the "Over-plus Land."

As the construction of the meeting house commenced in 1748, the settlers eagerly anticipated the growth of their community and the promise of a place where they could gather to worship, celebrate and build a future together in the heart of the breathtaking Mountains.

Wigwam Hill, named for its notable prominence, became the symbolic center of communal life. The meeting house, a testament to the settlers' unwavering faith, rose against the backdrop of the pristine landscape, a beacon of hope in the untamed wilderness. The sturdy beams of the structure bore witness to the aspirations and dreams of a community striving for unity and connection.

In the dwelling adjacent to the meeting house, Mr. Noah Mirick, the spiritual shepherd of the settlers, had his home, which was built in 1742. From this vantage point, he not only tended to the spiritual needs of the community but also became an integral part of their daily lives. His residence became a focal point for gatherings, discussions and solace, solidifying his role as a guiding force in the development of the settlement.

The location on Wigwam Hill, with its panoramic views of the surrounding landscape, provided a fitting setting for the meeting house and the minister's residence. As the community thrived, this hill became more than a physical elevation—it became a symbol of unity, strength and shared purpose.

The burying ground, a poignant reminder of life's transience, was designated by the village in 1736, a few years before the establishment of the meeting house on Wigwam Hill. Located at the foot of the hill on Over-plus Land, this sacred ground held the stories of those who shaped the destiny of the Mountains community.

Interestingly, the village had set aside this solemn space, displaying foresight in planning for the inevitable. However, the first recorded death did not occur until August 19, 1736, when the somber occasion of young David Jones's passing unfolded. His parents, David and Hannah Jones, faced a dilemma—the father, perhaps seeking a different resting place for his child, chose not to make David the first occupant of the newly consecrated burying ground. Consequently, David Jones found his final resting place at the old Springfield Cemetery, starting an unintentional tradition.

Two more lives were laid to rest in Springfield before the establishment of the Fourth Precinct in 1741. However, it was in that transformative year that the burying ground welcomed its first permanent resident. Elizabeth Cockril, a thirty-nine-year-old widow from Boston, passed away on April 26, 1741, while visiting her sister, the wife of Samuel Warner. Mr. Warner, though not a stonecutter, displayed a heartfelt commitment to preserving Elizabeth's memory. With two flat stones, he engraved her name and the date of her death, marking the initiation of the cemetery. Elizabeth's final resting place, adorned with those engraved stones, occupies the southeast quarter of the old section, a poignant beginning to a place that would hold the stories of generations to come.

As time unfolded in the Mountains community, the burying ground continued to bear witness to the passage of lives and the shared history of the settlers. In the mid-1700s, the cemetery became the final resting place for the three young children of Daniel Warner. The years 1746, 1748 and 1749 marked the somber occasions of their burials, each commemorated by a single stone that stood as a poignant testament to the fragility of life.

Through the years, the burying ground acquired various names, each reflecting a facet of its history and significance. It was known as the Burying Yard, the Old Yard and the Center Cemetery, capturing the essence of its role as a central space for communal remembrance. In time, the cemetery took on the name of Adams Cemetery, a nod to the Deacon Adams family, who left an indelible mark on the community. Their house, built just east of the cemetery on West Road (Main Street) in 1794, stands as a testament to their enduring legacy.

Situated off the West Road (Main Street), the burying ground held a central position in the community, a silent witness to the evolving landscape. Tinkham Road, now a familiar route, did not come into existence as a road until 1765. In a survey conducted in 1794, it was referenced as "the road from 16-Acres Mill to Wilbraham Street [Main Street] near the burying ground." This description underscored the significance of the cemetery as a landmark and a point of reference in the expanding settlement's roads and pathways.

The names engraved on the weathered stones told stories of joy and sorrow, of families and friendships. As the community continued to grow, the Adams Cemetery remained a poignant link to the past, a place where the threads of history and remembrance converged, weaving a narrative that spanned generations.

Adams Cemetery in 1964. *Wilbraham Public Library, Ives Collection.*

Over the years, the Adams Cemetery, once a modest resting place at the foot of Wigwam Hill, underwent a series of improvements that mirrored the evolving needs and care of the community. In 1805, a committee, appointed by the parish, took on the responsibility "to fence the Burying Ground near the street." The community recognized the importance of maintaining and protecting this sacred space. Two years later, in 1807, the parish granted permission for the fence to be painted, signifying a commitment to preserving the dignity and appearance of the cemetery.

Around 1859, a collective effort unfolded as a group of men from the town gathered to enhance the cemetery. Their mission included cutting back overgrown brush, improving the yard's overall appearance and conducting a thorough cleanup of the grounds. This collective endeavor not only showcased the communal spirit but also resulted in the realignment of some headstones and footstones along the southerly side, creating a more cohesive and organized layout.

As the community continued to grow, so did the need for additional resting places within the cemetery. In 1876, an expansion on the east side enlarged the original lot. Another significant addition occurred in 1896 when a much larger section was incorporated on the north side.

In 1969, recognizing the ongoing demand for burial space, further property was acquired on the east side, known as "New East." This expansion reinforced the commitment to accommodating the needs of the community, ensuring that the Adams Cemetery could continue to serve as a place of solace, remembrance and connection for generations to come.

The Adams Cemetery, with its storied history and continuous adaptations, stands as a testament to the resilience and reverence of the Mountains community, a living testament to the passage of time and the enduring ties that bind generations together.

The Adams Cemetery not only held the stories of those interred within its grounds but also bore witness to the changing customs and necessities of the community. For many years, a hearse house stood proudly at the southeast corner of the original lot, serving as a place to house the hearse—a solemn conveyance for the departed.

In 1871, recognizing the need for adjustments, the hearse house changed location. The decision was made to relocate it to the carriage shop near the north edge of the center village at 380 Main Street. This shift reflected a practical response to the evolving needs of the community, providing easier access to the hearse and ensuring a more efficient and centralized location for funeral preparations.

In 1876, the Town of Wilbraham assumed custodial care of the Adams Cemetery, along with two others: East Wilbraham Cemetery and Glendale Cemetery. This marked a significant shift in the responsibility for maintaining these sacred grounds, as the town took on the role of caretaker for these final resting places.

The Wilbraham Cemetery Commission (WCC) was established in 1919, embodying a more organized and dedicated approach to the management of the cemeteries. The commission comprised three elected members, with each member assigned to oversee a specific cemetery. This division of responsibilities allowed for a more focused and efficient administration of custodial care and maintenance.

Under the auspices of the Wilbraham Cemetery Commission, the Adams Cemetery, with its rich history and evolving landscape, continued to be cherished and preserved as a vital part of the community's heritage. The establishment of the commission underscored the town's commitment to ensuring the respectful and well-maintained condition of these burial grounds, recognizing their importance as historical, cultural and communal assets.

Around 1910, two generations of the Merrick family, namely Charles S. Merrick, the father, and Charles L. Merrick, his son, undertook the construction of a cement block building. This building, initially erected for a specific purpose, served as a pragmatic response to the challenges posed

Casket storage rack, circa 1910. *Atheneum Society of Wilbraham.*

by the winter months. Its primary function was to provide a storage facility for bodies during the colder seasons. As customs and practices evolved, and with the advancement of facilities and technologies, the original purpose of the cement block building changed. In more recent times, it has found a new role as an equipment shed.

A paranormal investigation conducted on September 28, 2013, at Adams Cemetery uncovered intriguing phenomena and captured evidence suggesting a connection to the historical and perhaps tragic events associated with the resting places within the cemetery.

Notably, audible recordings near the graves of Joseph Cutt and Caesar Mirick, African American slaves of the prominent Mirick family, revealed potential paranormal activity. These men, who had fought in the Revolutionary War alongside other Wilbraham soldiers, seemed to leave an imprint on the atmosphere, manifesting in audible recordings during the investigation.

A particularly compelling incident occurred at the site of the Bliss grave—three Bliss children met a tragic end in a drowning incident in 1799. Alongside them, three others were buried nearby. During the investigation, an investigator reported a tangible tug on his leg. A photograph taken at that very moment captured a gripping scene, showing an indentation on both

Adams Cemetery in 1964, with the Vault House in the background. *Wilbraham Public Library, Ives Collection.*

pant legs. This occurrence added a layer of intrigue to the site, hinting at a connection to the past and the tragic events that unfolded in town.

Throughout the evening, the investigators documented light streaks and intriguing orbs in black-and-white photos. These visual phenomena displayed definitive patterns emanating from various gravestones. The captured images suggested a dynamic interaction between the paranormal realm and the historical narratives embedded in the cemetery.

The paranormal investigation at Adams Cemetery not only shed light on potential supernatural activity but also unveiled a poignant connection to the historical events and figures buried within its grounds. The captured evidence and experiences added layers of mystery and depth to the cemetery, inviting further contemplation and exploration of stories from the past.

To support the ongoing maintenance and improvement efforts, the Town of Wilbraham has established a perpetual trust fund specifically designated for Adams, East Wilbraham and Glendale Cemeteries. This fund operates in a manner that only the interest income is utilized for the upkeep and enhancements, while the principal remains accumulated within the trust fund account. The careful management of this fund ensures a sustainable and enduring source of support for the cemeteries.

The Board of Cemetery Commissioners welcomes contributions of any amount to the perpetual trust fund, expressing gratitude for the support from the community. The commitment to transparency is evident, as each commissioner makes themselves available to discuss the details of the trust fund, fostering open communication with the community they serve.

The old section of Adams Cemetery—delineated from the east entrance road to the fence and Tinkham Road to the line of monuments in alignment with the old cemetery vault house—holds a significant historical presence. Within this area lie 995 headstones and foot markers, each telling a unique story and contributing to the rich history of the cemetery. The careful stewardship and community support ensure that Adams Cemetery continues to stand as a meaningful and well-maintained space for remembrance and reflection.

The historical gravestones at Adams Cemetery provide a fascinating glimpse into the evolving styles and materials used in memorializing the departed over the years. Up until the 1830s, brownstones sourced from local quarries in Wilbraham and elsewhere dominated the landscape of the cemetery. One such quarry, approximately 1,500 feet east of Adams Cemetery, likely supplied most of these brownstones that became the canvas for countless inscriptions and artistic expressions. The shift in materials after the 1830s introduced light-colored stones, such as white sandstone and marble. Slate stones from around 1870 and the later introduction of durable granite monuments marked further changes in the cemetery's aesthetic.

The variety of stones reflects different eras and tastes in memorialization. Brownstone markers from the early period often feature intricate carvings like "egg-headed angels," halos, cherubs, sunbursts and decorative elements such as interlacing vines, leaves, circles, wheels and flowers. After 1800, a shift in style is evident, with decorations adopting the imagery of weeping willows, urns and alterations in inscriptions and epitaphs.

Interestingly, some stones in the cemetery serve as cenotaphs, commemorating individuals who are buried elsewhere. This practice speaks to the desire to remember and honor individuals, even if their final resting places are beyond the cemetery grounds.

Beyond their aesthetic and historical significance, these gravestones provide valuable genealogical information. The inscriptions on the early stones, dating back 275 years or more, often offer more details about the individuals, their relationships and sometimes even personal attributes. The variations in spelling, even within the same family, highlight the historical nuances of language and naming conventions.

Adams Cemetery stands as not only a final resting place for the departed but also a repository of cultural and artistic expressions, reflecting the evolving styles and values of the Wilbraham community over the centuries. The gravestones serve as enduring markers, capturing the essence of lives lived and commemorating the diverse stories that make up the fabric of the community's history.

It's truly fascinating to learn about the rich history and connections surrounding Adams Cemetery and others, especially through the lens of Dr. Melvin G. Williams's book, *The Last Word*. The title alone hints at the intriguing exploration of early New England graveyards and the cultural significance embedded in their stones. Dr. Williams, an English professor at American International College in Springfield, emerged as a prominent figure in the study of early New England gravestones. His dedication to this field is evident in the wealth of knowledge he shared through his writings and lectures. The fact that sections of his book are related to Adams Cemetery adds a special layer of significance to the cemetery's cultural and historical importance.

The unique symbols on Dr. Williams's headstone in Adams Cemetery echo the tradition of early gravestones and serve as a fitting tribute to his expertise in this field. His contributions not only as an author but also as a speaker at historical societies and civic organizations highlight his commitment to sharing the allure and lore of these sacred grounds.

It's noteworthy that the book remains available online, allowing others to delve into the captivating world of early New England graveyards and the insights provided by Dr. Melvin G. Williams. His passing in 2004 marked the end of an era, but the enduring legacy of his work and his final resting place at Adams Cemetery continue to contribute to the appreciation and understanding of this unique aspect of New England's cultural heritage. In being a cemetery commissioner, you carry on the spirit of stewardship and preservation exemplified by individuals like Dr. Williams, connecting the past with the present and ensuring the legacy of these remarkable spaces endures.

THE FIRST CHURCH OF THE OUTWARD COMMONS

In the early eighteenth century, the Outward Commons of Springfield, nestled within the picturesque expanse of Ludlow, Wilbraham and Hampden today, stood as a testament to the resilience of pioneering settlers. This land, alternately known as Springfield Mountain or simply the Mountains, bore witness to the struggles and triumphs of a community determined to maintain their faith in the face of geographic challenges.

The settlers of this region found themselves confronted with a daunting journey of nine miles to attend religious services at the First Church in Springfield. The harsh winters, with biting cold and heavy snow, made this pilgrimage even more arduous. Undeterred by the inhospitable conditions, the community sought a solution that would both honor their commitment to worship and spare them from the harsh winter elements.

On January 3, 1739, Springfield granted a significant concession to the residents of the Mountains. Recognizing the difficulty of their situation, the town agreed to provide preaching for ten Sabbaths during the winter, each Sabbath earning the preachers a stipend of twenty shillings. This marked the beginning of a thoughtful arrangement that would repeat itself over the next two winters.

The settlers of the Outward Commons were saved from the treacherous journey to the Springfield settlement for religious services. The remote landscape of the Mountains became a haven for spiritual reflection during the cold months, as local preachers shared their wisdom with the grateful community.

As the years passed, the community thrived, and the Outward Commons that once seemed so isolated became integral parts of the expanding New England frontier. The story of these early settlers, their commitment to faith and the ingenious solution they found to overcome geographical barriers stands as a testament to the enduring spirit of community and resilience in the face of adversity.

In June 1740, the residents took a significant step by drafting a petition, a document that carried their hopes and aspirations for local governance and recognition. This petition was carefully presented to the General Court, the legislative body overseeing the Massachusetts Bay Colony.

The petition was not in vain, for on January 6, 1741, Governor Jonathan Belcher granted the request for the Outward Commons of Springfield in becoming the Fourth Precinct, which marked a pivotal moment in history. However, there was a discrepancy between the petition and the official grant. The petition encompassed all three divisions of the Outward Commons, but the grant did not mention most of the first division and part of the second division, which lies just north of the Chicopee River. Unfortunately this was entirely overlooked, and the Fourth Precinct, as officially established by the General Court, comprised the lands lying southward of the Chicopee River, encompassing what is now Wilbraham and Hampden.

The birth of the Fourth Precinct was followed by a momentous occasion on March 12, 1741—the inaugural precinct meeting. This historic gathering unfolded at the residence of David Merrick, a settler who had made his home on West Road around 1735, now identified as 515 Main Street in Wilbraham. In the midst of this community meeting, precinct officers were duly elected, setting the stage for the governance and growth of the newly established precinct.

Over the course of the next few months, leading up to June, six distinct meetings were convened. Among these, the gathering on April 17, 1741, proved particularly significant. During this meeting, the precinct officers "unanimously voted a Call or Desire" for the esteemed Mr. Noah Merrick to settle with them "in the work of the Ministry." This gesture underscored the importance of religious leadership within the community and demonstrated a commitment to fostering a strong spiritual foundation for the evolving precinct.

The unfolding events of 1741 brought not only the establishment of the Fourth Precinct but also a significant development in the spiritual leadership of the burgeoning community. In a letter dated May 26, 1741, from

Springfield, Mr. Noah Merrick expressed his acceptance of the invitation extended to him by the precinct. The terms were clear and reflective of the community's commitment to ensuring the well-being of their chosen spiritual guide.

Mr. Merrick agreed to the position with a compensation package that included a salary or other commodities equivalent to one hundred pounds per year. Additionally, a residence was to be constructed for him, and land would be allocated from the over-plus land in the middle division. This arrangement spoke to the practical considerations of providing for the spiritual leader and reflected the shared commitment of the community to supporting their religious foundation.

By 1742, the community had fulfilled its promise, and a splendid home was erected for Reverend Noah Merrick on Wigwam Hill. In the modern context, this location aligns in the area of 1347 Tinkham Road in Wilbraham. The completion of this residence not only provided a home for the minister but also served as a tangible symbol of the community's dedication to their spiritual leader.

Adding a personal touch to this significant chapter in their lives, Reverend Merrick took another noteworthy step in October 1744. He married Abigail Brainard of Haddam, Connecticut. The newlyweds, on their journey home to the minister's house, carried with them slips of a rose bush from Abigail's family home. Upon arrival, Abigail planted these slips, ensuring that the blossoms of this rose bush would become a part of their new home on Springfield Mountain.

This gesture, seemingly small, carried a profound significance, marking the union of two lives and the intertwining of their personal histories with the budding history of the community. The story of Reverend Noah Merrick, his home on Wigwam Hill and the planting of the rose bush stands as a poignant reminder of the personal and communal threads that weave the tapestry of history in the Outward Commons.

The saga of establishing a meeting house in the Fourth Precinct unfolded over nearly seven years, a testament to the challenges and deliberations faced by the community. The process was marked by intense debates and considerations over the optimal location for this central gathering place, a decision that would shape the communal and religious life of the Outward Commons.

The initial proposal involved situating the meeting house on the "Green," identified as West Road in contemporary terms (today's 678 Main Street, Wilbraham). This location likely symbolized a central point for the community, a hub where residents could come together for both religious and civic purposes.

The second contender for the meeting house site was Pine Hill, an area that corresponds to present-day Echo Hill Road in Wilbraham. This elevation may have offered some scenic views, but the practical considerations and the desires of the community ultimately led to further deliberations.

The third and final location considered was Wigwam Hill, situated near the residence of Reverend Noah Merrick, at the current address just south of 1339 Tinkham Road, Wilbraham. This spot, with its proximity to the minister's home, held symbolic significance and may have facilitated the involvement of the congregation in the life of their spiritual leader.

After much debate, Wigwam Hill emerged as the chosen site for the meeting house. By late 1748, construction was underway, and the meeting house began to take shape. In its initial stages, the building served as a mere shell, reflecting the gradual progress of the community's efforts. The views to the west from this location were breathtaking, as one could see the entire Connecticut River Valley below.

Recognizing the importance of completing this central structure, the community voted in January 1752 to further finish the meeting house. This decision marked a significant step in providing a more functional and comfortable space for religious gatherings, community meetings and other communal activities. The meeting house, now firmly established on Wigwam Hill, became a focal point for the residents, representing the collective spirit and determination that characterized the early development of the Outward Commons.

The evolution of Wilbraham's governance and religious landscape continued to unfold in the years following its incorporation in 1763. By 1782, the town had grown sufficiently to warrant the division into two parishes for religious services: the North Parish and the South Parish. Notably, the South Parish eventually became the town of Hampden in 1878.

In the South Parish, a meeting house was erected in the village along the Scantic River, where the Civil War Monument stands today, providing a central location for religious gatherings and community events. Meanwhile, the original meeting house on Wigwam Hill in the North Parish now faced a changing landscape.

With the establishment of two parishes, the need for the meeting house on Wigwam Hill diminished. A decision was reached to relocate the building to a more central location within the North Parish. However, the process of determining whether to move the existing meeting house or construct a new one, as well as selecting the precise location, became a subject of prolonged debate.

After twelve years of deliberation, a vote in 1794 settled the matter. It was decided to move the Old Meeting House off Wigwam Hill and temporarily position it in the middle of Wilbraham Street, in front of what is now 500 Main Street. This temporary placement was intended to last for two or three weeks until a permanent location could be determined.

Interestingly, the brief stay of the meeting house in the middle of the street had lasting effects on the town's infrastructure. The width of Main Street in front of the present-day United Church may owe its unusual dimensions to this historical episode. During the temporary relocation, travelers navigated around both sides of the building, contributing to the shaping of the surrounding road layout.

The decision-making process regarding the meeting house's location continued to be contentious, with some members of the parish expressing a desire for the building to remain in its temporary location on Wilbraham Street. This period of transition and debate underscores the dynamic nature of community development in early American history, where decisions about religious and civic structures played a central role in shaping the identity and landscape of growing towns like Wilbraham.

The story of Charles Brewer and the relocation of the meeting house adds a fascinating layer to the history of Wilbraham. Charles Brewer, originally a Congregationalist, played a pivotal role in the community's religious landscape. In an interesting turn of events, Charles Brewer became the first to be baptized in the original meeting house on Wigwam Hill on December 25, 1748. However, as the community evolved and discussions unfolded regarding the relocation of the meeting house, Brewer found himself at the center of a crucial decision.

In 1791, a vote was taken to move the meeting house from its hilltop location to a more central spot in town. The chosen parcel of land for this relocation was donated by Brewer. However, just three weeks later, the vote was rescinded, leading to Brewer's decision to withdraw from the First Parish along with twelve others. This withdrawal marked the formation of the Methodist Society, highlighting the denominational diversity and religious dynamics within the community.

In 1793, Charles Brewer offered the same property on Wilbraham Street (450 Main Street today) to the Methodist Society for the construction of its meeting house. In a unique lease agreement, Brewer stipulated an annual rent of one peppercorn, a symbolic and nominal amount. This interesting historical detail is documented in the lease.

Today, the Atheneum Society of Wilbraham occupies the building, with the town owning the land and building. The annual lease, set at one peppercorn, is a living testament to the historical agreement forged between Charles Brewer and the Methodist Society.

Ultimately, the Congregational Meeting House, having served a stint in the middle of the road, found its permanent location at what is now Gazebo Park on Main Street in the center of town. This relocation marked not only a physical move but also a symbolic shift in the religious and communal landscape of Wilbraham, capturing the spirit of compromise, community development and religious diversity.

From the death of Reverend Noah Merrick on December 25, 1776, there was no settled minister until May 23, 1787, when Reverend Joseph Willard was installed. He was dismissed on February 11, 1794, after serving nearly seven years.

The ministry of Reverend Ezra Witter, spanning from August 16, 1797, to May 31, 1814, marked a period of growth and renewal for the community in Wilbraham. One notable accomplishment during this time was the repair of the Old Meeting House, a central place of worship for the town.

In 1802, under Reverend Witter's leadership, the community took a significant step by purchasing and hanging a church bell. This event holds particular historical significance as it marked the introduction of "the first Sabbath bell of the Mountains." The presence of a church bell not only served a practical purpose in signaling the start of religious services but also symbolized a sense of permanence and community identity.

Other ministers had served this church until 1911:

- Reverend Ebenezer Brown, 1819–27
- Reverend John Hyde, 1828–31
- Reverend Israel G. Rose, 1832–35
- Reverend John Bowers, 1837–56
- Reverend John P. Skeele, 1857–64
- Reverend Alexander D. Stowell, 1865–67
- Reverend Martin S. Howard, 1868–1911

The Old Meeting House, which had witnessed decades of history, was moved to what is now Burt Lane in 1857 and converted into a horse shed.

In its place, a more spacious and architecturally impressive structure was erected, becoming a central point in the community.

However, tragedy struck on Sunday, June 24, 1877, when a devastating fire consumed the second meeting house and several buildings in the center village, including the Old Meeting House/horse shed. According to reports, the fire originated from the actions of a mischievous boy who, in a moment of recklessness, ignited papers in a stove in the basement of the church that lacked a connected chimney pipe.

In the aftermath of the fire, the Congregationalists found themselves without a place of worship. The Methodist Society, with its brownstone church just north on Main Street, demonstrated a remarkable act of generosity and community spirit. It voted to invite the Congregational brethren to use its church for worship until the Congregational church could be rebuilt.

From July 1, 1877, to August 26, 1877, the two societies worshiped together, and the ministers from each denomination alternated in the preaching. Following this period of joint worship, the two societies held separate services until February 3, 1878. This period of shared worship and cooperation was a historic turning point, marking the first time in eighty-five years that the two churches, once characterized by rivalry and discord, found common ground and acceptance of each other.

The fire that brought destruction also became an unexpected catalyst for unity, illustrating the resilience and communal spirit of the people of Wilbraham. The willingness of the Methodist Society to open its doors to its Congregational neighbors fostered a newfound understanding and cooperation that transcended religious differences, leading to a more harmonious relationship between the two churches.

The construction and dedication of the third meeting house in Wilbraham in 1878 marked a significant moment in the town's history, especially considering the recent challenges faced due to the destructive fire. This new building, erected on the same property where its predecessors stood, represented a renewal and a commitment to the community's spiritual and communal life.

Dedicated on June 26, 1878, the third meeting house was an elaborate structure, surpassing its predecessors in architectural detail. It featured two spires, with the main one described as "very high and graceful." Two tower entrances from the street added to its grandeur, creating a welcoming and impressive façade. A large rose window on the north side of the building added a touch of beauty and symbolism, likely serving as a tribute to Abigail Merrick, the wife of the first minister, Reverend Noah Merrick.

The third Congregational Church, 1878–1911. *Wilbraham Public Library.*

A notable feature of the new meeting house was its bell, weighing 1,662 pounds. This bell incorporated a part of the old bell, generously given by Ethan C. Ely of Longmeadow. Ely donated the bell in memory of his family, who had lived in Wilbraham, creating a link between the past and the present.

The construction and dedication of this new meeting house not only provided the community with a place of worship but also stood as a testament to the resilience and unity of the people of Wilbraham. The elaborate design and incorporation of historical elements reflected a commitment to both the spiritual and architectural heritage of the town, marking a new chapter in the continuing story of Wilbraham's religious and communal life.

The unfortunate fire that struck this third meeting house on July 5, 1911, dealt another devastating blow to the congregants of Wilbraham. This calamity, sparked by a lightning strike during a passing wind and electrical storm, began at the pinnacle of the highest spire and consumed the entire building in its destructive path.

Facing the loss of their place of worship yet again, the Congregationalists found themselves in need of a temporary location. In a gesture reminiscent of the past, the Methodists stepped in to offer their place of worship in the brownstone stone church. This act of generosity demonstrated a continued spirit of community and shared understanding between the two congregations, echoing the cooperative efforts seen in previous instances of adversity.

The fire not only physically devastated this third meeting house but also tested the resilience and unity of the community. The shared history of the Congregationalists and Methodists, bound by mutual support during times of crisis, stood as a testament to the enduring strength of the Wilbraham community in the face of challenges.

The construction of the fourth meeting house in Wilbraham marked a departure from the elaborate designs of its predecessors. This gray shingled building with white trim and a slate roof was a simpler structure, reflecting the practical and economic considerations of its time. It was dedicated on May 11, 1913, at a cost of $17,000.

In 1916, a new bell was cast and installed, incorporating metal salvaged from the old bells. This new bell was a gift from Mrs. Lucia S. Foskit and Mrs. Laura H. Bruuer, a thoughtful contribution that added a touch of continuity to the rebuilt church.

The reconstruction and subsequent use of the fourth meeting house marked a significant point in the history of Wilbraham's religious community. The joint efforts of both Congregationalists and Methodists demonstrated a unity that had evolved over the years, particularly in times of rebuilding and shared worship spaces.

A practical arrangement was established for the shared usage of the two churches. From May 1 to October 31, the Methodist church was utilized, and from November 1 to April 30, the Congregational church took precedence. This shared usage extended beyond religious services; social activities were

The fourth Congregational Church, 1912–58. *Wilbraham Public Library.*

primarily conducted in the Congregational church, thanks to its additional facilities like a dining room and kitchen.

This period of shared facilities and cooperative efforts represented a new chapter in the history of the Wilbraham community, emphasizing unity and collaboration between the Congregationalists and Methodists. The fourth meeting house, with its simpler design and shared usage, became a symbol of the enduring strength and unity of the town's religious community.

The year 1941 brought a significant change to the religious landscape of Wilbraham. The Methodist Society church, constructed of brownstone, was transferred to Wilbraham Academy. This decision was influenced by a decline in the number of worshipers, prompting a restructuring of the available church facilities.

In addition to the transfer of the church building, the parsonage associated with the Methodist Society was also transferred to Wilbraham United Church. These moves marked a shift in the organizational structure and physical presence of the religious communities in Wilbraham.

With both the Congregationalists and Methodists now under one roof, the shared facilities became a symbol of unity and cooperation within the town. The consolidation of resources and spaces reflected the evolving dynamics of the religious communities in response to changing demographics and worship patterns.

In 1949, a significant renovation and expansion project took place in the sanctuary. The space underwent a complete remodeling, and an ell wing was added to accommodate educational activities. This expansion allowed for a more versatile use of the building, providing enhanced facilities for educational programs and community engagement.

The culmination of these changes was marked by the dedication of the enlarged building on April 30, 1950. This event not only celebrated the physical enhancements to the church but also symbolized the continued unity and collaborative spirit of the Wilbraham religious community, now united under one roof.

The construction of a new colonial brick church by Wilbraham United Church in 1958 marked another chapter in the town's religious history. Situated just south of its previous location at 500 Main Street, this new building was dedicated on March 23, 1958. The colonial architectural style added a distinctive touch to the town's landscape, reflecting both tradition and a sense of continuity.

The old Congregational building, the previous location of Wilbraham United Church, continued to serve a purpose even after the construction of the new church. It became a venue for dinners and various social activities, contributing to the continued sense of community that had been a hallmark of Wilbraham's religious life.

Additionally, the old Congregational building found a new purpose when a newly formed Episcopal Church group began using it for worship. This shared usage demonstrated a spirit of cooperation and openness among different religious denominations in Wilbraham.

However, this period of shared worship and community activities in the old building came to an end in December 1962 when the structure was razed. The changing landscape, both physically and symbolically, reflected the evolving needs and dynamics of the religious community in Wilbraham during this era. The construction of the new colonial brick church and the eventual removal of the old building marked a transformative period in the town's religious history, embodying a balance between tradition and adaptation to contemporary needs.

The Wilbraham United Church continues to thrive and play an active role in the community, embodying a unique and inclusive spirit. The congregation's history of merging the Congregational and Methodist Societies since 1913 speaks to a longstanding commitment to unity and collaboration.

The congregation's decision to draw from the traditions and values of both the United Church of Christ and the United Methodist denominations is a testament to its open-minded and inclusive approach. Celebrating diversity and promoting a sense of unity through this blend of traditions reflects a community that embraces different perspectives and backgrounds.

The emphasis on love as the most important value resonates with the teachings of both denominations, highlighting the shared emphasis on compassion and care for others. Valuing wisdom and laughter equally suggests a well-rounded understanding of spirituality, acknowledging the importance of both seriousness and joy in the faith journey.

The commitment to active engagement in service and community-building activities demonstrates a desire to live out the principles of love and compassion in practical ways. This holistic approach to spirituality, integrating worship with a focus on service and community, fosters a vibrant and supportive environment for the members.

It's inspiring to see how this congregation has evolved over the years, navigating changes while staying true to its core values. The unity, inclusivity and commitment to service make it a dynamic and thriving community that continues to impact the lives of its members and the broader Wilbraham community.

MASTERS OF STONE AND TIME

CHRONICLES OF THE PIONEERING GRAVESTONE ARTISANS

During the seventeenth and eighteenth centuries, the towns located along the Connecticut River in Western Massachusetts formed a unique region within the Bay Colony. While these towns were part of Massachusetts politically, they were separated from Boston by more than eighty miles of sparsely populated hill country. Due to the distance and rugged terrain, the Massachusetts river towns had closer ties to Connecticut. From the beginning of settlement, family ties, trade and communication bound the settlers of Western Massachusetts to residents of Windsor, Hartford and Wethersfield, Connecticut. Despite this, connections to Boston were preserved through kinship, politics and commerce, growing in importance during the eighteenth century. The combination of political development and geography produced a cultural region in the river towns of Western Massachusetts, which, despite its relative isolation, was open to influences from both the Bay area and Connecticut, occasionally producing its distinctive artistic expressions. Surviving gravestones in the region are a testament to this cultural and artistic heritage.

During the 1740s, a large number of cherub stones with intricate foliate borders appeared in Old Hampshire County (Hampden County). These stones were carved by Thomas Johnson II (1718–1774), Joseph Johnson (1698–circa 1770), William Holland (working 1748–67) and Nathaniel Phelps (1721–1789). The resemblance between the stones was due to the master-apprentice relationships between these cutters. Thomas Johnson II, his uncle Joseph Johnson and Gideon Hale all trained with Thomas Johnson

I in Middletown, and even though Joseph worked in East Windsor during much of the 1740s, the Middletown sandstone quarries remained the focal point for the family. William Holland worked for Joseph Johnson in East Windsor in 1748 and may have been trained by him, as he returned with Joseph to Middletown around 1750.

Along the east bank of the Connecticut River, from South Hadley to Longmeadow, families purchased grave markers from the Johnsons. The Johnsons supplied most of the gravestones placed in these towns during the late 1740s and early 1750s. William Holland moved from Middletown to Longmeadow (East Longmeadow) in 1756 to take advantage of this market. He bought land and began producing grave markers in locally quarried stone. Holland was an extremely skillful carver and spent most of his career as a journeyman working for others and in their styles. However, several distinctive gravestones in Connecticut can be documented to be his work, revealing that his status as a journeyman had nothing to do with his talent as a stonecutter or "stone carver," as he called himself. During his three- to four-year stay in Longmeadow, he was his own master and produced stones with his distinct touches. The low hairy foreheads, the precise lettering and the hooked numeral "1" recall his earlier work and that of his probable master, Joseph Johnson. However, the languid, open foliate borders, the crown surmounted by a globe and the Maltese cross are innovations of Holland. The use of the cross may explain why Holland placed only a few stones outside of Longmeadow in neighboring Springfield; the mid-Connecticut River Valley was probably not ready for such a papist symbol. Holland left Longmeadow at some time in 1760 and returned to the Middletown area, where he cut stones with his distinctive pointed crowns that can be seen in Durham, Middletown, North Guilford and North Haven, Connecticut graveyards. He stopped working in the late 1760s and vanished without a trace.

Holland's influence had a lasting impact on southern Hampshire County, even after he left. It seems that he trained two or three stonecutters from the Springfield area. Joseph Williston (1732–68) of Springfield produced about one hundred gravestones in red sandstone between 1759 and 1767. Williston imitated Holland's lettering, borders and effigies but changed some things. He didn't add hair on the forehead and only carved three stones with crosses. His work was somewhat stiffer, smaller and simpler compared to Holland's. He beautified at least four of his stones by carving a brick wall under the effigy. He placed most of his stones in South Hadley, Springfield, West Springfield and Westfield, and some examples are found in Chicopee, Deerfield, Hadley, Hatfield and Northampton. Nathaniel Phelps, who produced only a few stones during the mid-1760s, had been the primary supplier for the last four towns mentioned. Unfortunately, Williston's career was cut short by his untimely death, but it seemed to have been promising.

After Williston's death, Aaron Bliss (1739–76) of Wilbraham supplied Williston's market. Aaron Bliss called himself a stonecutter, and his probate inventory contained four stone axes, four hewing chisels, nine writing chisels, two iron claws, an iron mallet, an iron sledge and a pair of compasses. A man of modest circumstances, Bliss supplemented his income from stonecutting by blacksmithing. He appears to have begun cutting gravestones in the later 1760s in a dark-brown sandstone easily distinguished from the red sandstone used by Williston and the paler, closer-grained brown sandstone used by the Longmeadow stonecutter. His stones usually had winged cherubs and foliate borders that recall the work of Holland and Joseph Johnson. Most of Bliss's stones, including those that mark his children's graves, are in Wilbraham; several are in Westfield, and examples can be found in South Hadley, Springfield, West Springfield and northern Connecticut. His death brought a temporary halt to stonecutting in Wilbraham, and when activity resumed in the 1780s under the direction of John Buckland (1749–93) of East Hartford, it marked a break with the traditions derived from Holland's work. At some point in time, Buckland moved to Wilbraham. His work was considered crude compared to Bliss and Stebbins.

The first tenant of the burying ground in the Outward Commons (Adams Cemetery, Wilbraham) was thirty-nine-year-old Elizabeth Cockril, who died on April 26, 1741. Elizabeth, who was a widow from Boston, was on a visit to her sister, who was Samuel Warner's wife, and became ill and died. Mr. Warner buried her here, and even though he was not a stonecutter, he found two flat brownstones and engraved her name and the date of her death; that was the first grave located in that cemetery. Her stones are located in the southeast quarter of the old section.

The influence of William Holland endured significantly in Longmeadow long after his departure. Following Holland's exit, a skilled stonecutter, evidently trained by him, continued crafting crowned cherubs that closely resembled Holland's work. However, these Longmeadow cherubs displayed broader proportions and less intricate detailing than Holland's originals. A plausible candidate for this Longmeadow stonecutter is Ezra Stebbins (1731–1796), a local gravestone maker. Stebbins, identified in the Stebbins family genealogy, received payments for gravestones in 1773 and 1784. The

Above, left: Gravestone in Adams Cemetery, Wilbraham, by stonecutter Aaron Bliss.
David F. Bourcier.

Above, right: Gravestone in Adams Cemetery, Wilbraham, by stonecutter John Buckland.
David F. Bourcier.

Opposite: Gravestone in Adams Cemetery, Wilbraham, by stonecutter Ebenezer Stebbins.
David F. Bourcier.

1773 payment may have been for the creation of the Mary Bliss stone from 1757 in Longmeadow.

Ebenezer Stebbins was another family member who was a stonecutter, along with many others in his family and extended families. He is credited for being the stone carver for all of the victims of the 1799 Nine Mile Pond tragedy. These gravestones are all in Adams Cemetery, Wilbraham.

Adams Cemetery has upward of 90 percent of the carved stones done by local stonecutters. Here are three more stonecutters who have at least one stone done by their hands: William Holland, Solomon Brewier and John Ely.

Despite the uncertainty surrounding the Longmeadow stonecutter's identity, it became evident that the crosses characteristic of Holland's work were abandoned. Eventually, even the distinctive hairy foreheads were phased out. In the late 1760s and 1770s, the Longmeadow shop transitioned to richly symbolic motifs such as hourglasses, crowing cocks and flowers cut

by scythes. Moving into the 1780s and 1790s, the shop expanded its repertoire to include portrait stones and crowned cherubs. These later cherubs, while reminiscent of the 1760s style, had distinguishing features.

The production of profile stones and crowned cherubs persisted beyond the death of Ezra Stebbins in 1796, possibly carried on by Ezra Stebbins II (1760–1819) of Longmeadow. Under the leadership of Herman Newell (1774–1833), the Longmeadow shop continued its gravestone production until the 1820s.

In towns where a preference for sandstone gravestones persisted, the urn and willow motifs experienced a delayed and often brief resurgence during the 1810s and 1820s. Notably, the stonecutters in Longmeadow and others working with sandstone in the Springfield area continued to offer gravestones adorned with motifs that, in many instances, directly descended from William Holland's designs in the 1750s.

Until about 1810, an artisan emulating the Sikes family's distinctive style remained active, supplying residents of Granby, South Hadley and Wilbraham with sandstone imitations of the Sikes family's unique effigies.

There were two brownstone quarries in Wilbraham that we know of: the Burt Quarry off Main Street and a smaller quarry off Stony Hill Road near Hitchcock Road. Most of the brownstone foundations and building stones come from the quarry off of Main Street and the rest from the Stony Hill Road property. The quarry off Stony Hill Road was abandoned before 1885. Some of the foundations in South Wilbraham (Hampden) came from the Main Street quarry in Wilbraham or the McGregory Quarry off Somers Road in East Longmeadow. An interesting note on the 1917 *Edson's Historical Map* shows the quarry located off Main Street belonging to McGregory at some point and also shows many stonecutter houses along Tinkham Road.

ANCIENT SAFEGUARDS

DECODING THE ENIGMA OF APOTROPAIC MARKS ACROSS WANDERING AGES

In the quaint town of Wilbraham, nestled within historic houses that stand as silent witnesses to centuries past, mysterious apotropaic marks (from Greek *apotrepein*, "to ward off") serve as symbols or patterns scratched into buildings or other objects to keep witches away through magic. These symbols grace walls, doors and attic beams alike. Known by many names, one common mark—called hexafoils, witch marks, six-petaled rosettes or six-lobed stars—have sparked curiosity and speculation across the globe.

Crafted with precision, often using compasses or carpenters' dividers, these symbols feature an outer circle embracing six pointed "petals," resembling an intricate flower. Their presence is not confined to Wilbraham; rather, they can be found in New England and beyond, adorning not just houses but also barns, furniture and gravestones. Yet their meaning remains shrouded in mystery, inviting theories as diverse as the symbols themselves.

Some insist that these marks are protective inscriptions against witches, a testament to the lingering fears that permeated seventeenth- and eighteenth-century New England. In an era marked by witch trials and supernatural anxieties, the belief in warding off malevolent forces persisted, prompting the use of symbols for spiritual fortification.

As whispers of witchcraft faded from popular consciousness in the mid-1800s, the daisy wheels endured, perhaps transformed into symbols of good luck and house blessings. Beyond their utilitarian origins, these symbols became cherished charms, adorning gravestones, Pennsylvania German barns, furniture and woodworking tools. Their persistence as

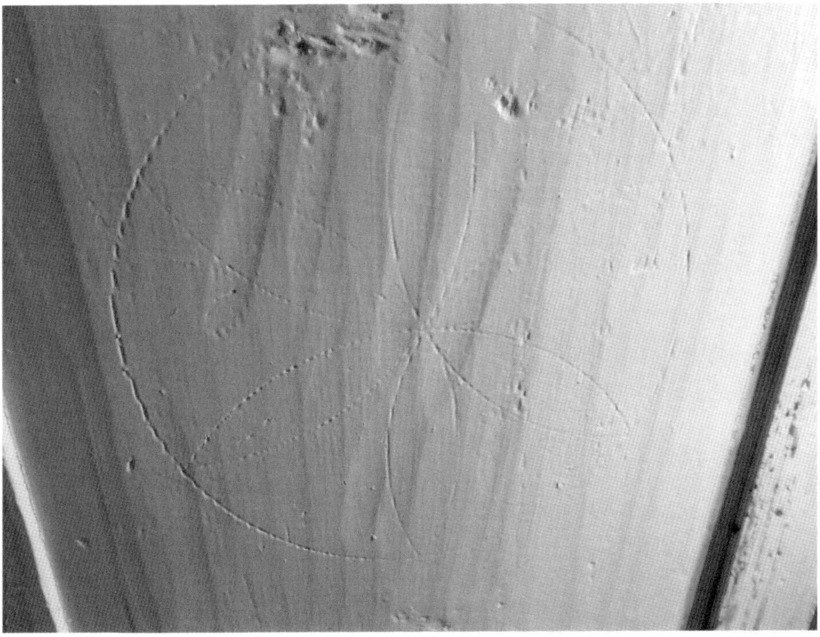

Daisy wheel, at the 1745 Abel Bliss House. *Bill Steele.*

attractive embellishments hints at a cultural continuity that transcends time and belief systems.

Exploring this unique history, daisy wheels are often found clustered around fireplaces, windows and doors, emphasizing the vulnerability of these openings. In England and the United States, they share spaces with other protective markings—fylfot, the evil eye, Marian marks—creating a mosaic of spiritual defense against unseen forces.

The daisy wheel phenomenon extends beyond mere markings; ritual deposits hidden within walls or under thresholds—worn shoes, animal skulls or iron implements—add a layer of mystique to the narrative. These concealed offerings, like a secret pact with the supernatural, further deepen the connection between the material and spiritual realms.

The second prevailing theory proposes that carpenters were responsible for creating daisy wheels, utilizing these intricate geometric symbols for measuring and designing during the construction process. This theory finds merit in the integration of geometric shapes and proportions in the architecture of even common buildings, necessitating master builders to possess a solid grasp of basic geometry and calculation skills, as they often played the dual role of architect and designer for vernacular structures.

Some researchers have attempted to validate this theory by superimposing daisy wheels onto scaled-down, measured drawings of buildings, revealing intriguing correlations with framing members and other architectural elements. It is noteworthy that builders did occasionally use building parts to sketch makeshift architectural plans or make calculations, as evidenced by scratched or chalked drawings found during restoration work on the backs of wallboards or the undersides of stair treads.

Builders—being well equipped with tools such as carpenters' dividers, race knives or compasses—were particularly adept at creating circular designs. Additionally, builders had access to various building parts, including elevated posts or beams in attics, that would be challenging for anyone to reach after construction. These spaces often contain carpenters' marks and lumber tally marks, sometimes mistaken for apotropaic markings.

Despite the appeal of attributing daisy wheels to house wrights, challenges emerge. Eighteenth-century architecture books, while discussing geometry and design with illustrations of geometric shapes, do not portray or explain daisy wheels in the construction context. Furthermore, the execution of many daisy wheels raises questions about their association with builders. Some were created long after construction, evident from multiple layers of paint, and are often found on highly visible, finished surfaces—a departure from the typical behavior of a careful carpenter.

The inconsistent quality of daisy wheels—marked by incorrect proportions, an unsteady hand or the use of suboptimal tools—challenges assumptions about carpenters' expertise and the supposed need for accurate, proportional daisy wheels for design purposes. Addressing these discrepancies is crucial in unraveling the true origin and purpose of these enigmatic symbols.

The third theory suggests that numerous daisy wheels may be whimsical creations, crafted by young adults or even children. It's essential to recognize the playful nature of historical individuals, acknowledging that they, too, experienced boredom and took pleasure in crafting aesthetically pleasing things. These captivating sketches from centuries past might be akin to the popular Spirograph drawing toy of the twentieth century. This notion could also account for the diverse array of compass-drawn circular symbols, which occasionally evolved beyond simple daisy wheels into intricate, interlocking designs involving numerous circles and arcs.

In some instances, a single dwelling might showcase myriad circular designs, ranging from concentric circles to daisy wheels and extending to clusters of plain circles or even elaborate wreaths and chains formed with a compass. These circular motifs often coexist with other playful graffiti,

Two daisy wheels, Ezra Barker's 1801 grave, Adams Cemetery, Wilbraham. *David F. Bourcier.*

such as carvings depicting people, buildings or animals.

However, it would be a misjudgment to dismiss daisy wheels and other marks as mere frivolous doodles, even when they are likely created as such. I contend that these markings hold significance for various reasons, contributing a meaningful layer to many historic sites. They serve as poignant reminders of the genuine connections people shared with the places they inhabited, akin to other historical symbols.

The daisy wheel—when observed in mortuary settings, engraved on gravestones or incorporated into burial practices—can be interpreted as a symbol signifying both the safeguarding of the departed soul and the protection of their earthly remains. This mystical tradition originated in the British Isles, spread throughout Europe, and eventually found its way to the colonial settlements of North America.

Although not the most prevalent motif on early colonial gravestones, the daisy wheel appears with sufficient frequency to warrant attention. Its presence suggests a deep-rooted connection to the history of graves and the protection of the deceased, a tradition that likely predates the advent of Christianity. In essence, the daisy wheel symbol has endured for centuries, and its association with the safeguarding of the dead is a testament to its enduring significance.

The daisy wheel not only graces the gravestones of colonial burial grounds but also boasts a rich history that spans across continents and civilizations. While many instances of the daisy wheel on graves likely served as apotropaic symbols for protection, it is conceivable that some later examples held different meanings. The allure of this symbol and other types of apotropaic marks lies in its extensive and captivating history, both in New England and around the world.

So, if you live in a historical home or even are venturing out to a local graveyard, look around. You may find a daisy wheel or other types of apotropaic marks for yourself. I would like to think of these as symbols of good luck.

UNVEILING THE UNTOLD TALE OF WILBRAHAM'S INCOMPLETE MEMORIAL TOWN HALL

In the early to mid-1800s, discussions about constructing a town hall had become a recurring theme on the town warrants. The idea was first proposed in 1838, and in 1840, the town warrant explicitly mentioned building a town house on the green near the residence of John Adams. This proposed location, now identified as 678 Main Street, is the current site of the Children's Museum.

However, during this period, the town was divided into the North and South Parishes, and the ongoing parish rivalry proved to be a significant obstacle in realizing the construction of a town hall. The proposed project faced continuous resistance and was repeatedly blocked from moving forward. Despite the town's evident need for a central gathering place, the divisions within the community prevented any substantial progress.

The situation changed in 1878 when the South Parish separated to form the independent town of Hampden. This event marked a significant turning point in the town's history, as the removal of parish divisions seemingly fostered a more unified community.

Seven years later, in 1885, the April town meeting included a pivotal article that reignited the discussion about building a town hall. The article read, "Voted: To build a Town Hall on the Green near the home of John Adams, as proposed in the 1840 Town Warrant." This time, the atmosphere was different; with the absence of parish rivalry, the residents were more inclined to support the construction of a central civic space.

The subsequent steps involved in planning, designing and constructing the town hall would become part of the town's ongoing narrative. The approved project not only addressed a practical need for a central meeting place but also served as a tangible expression of unity and community identity. The town hall would go on to play a central role in the town's social and civic life, becoming a historic landmark with its roots embedded in the decades-long journey from discussion to realization.

The proposed Article 16, presented during a town meeting, called for the consideration of erecting a monument in honor of the men from Wilbraham who lost their lives in the war for the preservation of the Union. The key components of Article 16 were as follows:

- Monument for Fallen Soldiers: The primary objective of the article was to discuss and decide on the erection of a building. This memorial building was intended to serve as a lasting tribute to the memory of the local men who made the ultimate sacrifice during the war for the preservation of the Union.
- Appropriations: The article proposed that the town vote on making all necessary appropriations to fund the construction of the memorial building. This implies that there would be a financial commitment from the town to support the project.
- Committee Formation: Additionally, the article suggested the formation of a committee to oversee and execute the project. This committee would likely be responsible for various aspects, including design selection and construction coordination, ensuring that the memorial building appropriately honored the fallen soldiers.

The significance of this article goes beyond its procedural aspects. It reflects the town's collective desire to honor and remember those who gave their lives in service to their country. Commemorative monuments like these serve as important symbols of gratitude, remembrance and a shared commitment to preserving the memory of the sacrifices made by members of the community during times of conflict. The outcome of the vote on this article would determine whether the town would proceed with the project and take steps to create a meaningful and lasting tribute to its fallen heroes.

Following the approval of Article 16 and the subsequent formation of a committee, the committee, comprising five individuals, diligently worked on outlining the details of the proposed monument. About one month after being tasked with this responsibility, the committee presented its findings and recommendations to the town.

The committee's report advocated for the construction of a memorial town hall, suggesting that it be situated in the Center Village, the very location where the current Civil War Monument stands today. This strategic placement would likely enhance the visibility and accessibility of the memorial, making it a central focus for the community.

Moreover, the proposed memorial town hall was intended to serve a dual purpose. Beyond its functional role as a town hall, the building was envisioned to be a lasting tribute to the memory of the men from Wilbraham who sacrificed their lives during the Civil War. This concept elevated the town hall from being a mere administrative structure to a meaningful and commemorative space, symbolizing the town's gratitude and remembrance for the sacrifices made by its residents.

The subsequent steps in the process—including securing funding, finalizing the design and overseeing the construction—would likely have been additional tasks for the committee. Following the approval, the committee took practical steps to implement the project. One crucial decision was the purchase of a suitable lot for the construction of the memorial town hall. The committee identified a plot of land owned by James B. Crane and negotiated its acquisition for $500. Notably, Zenas Crane, James's brother, generously contributed by paying half of the cost as a gift to the town.

This financial contribution by Zenas Crane demonstrated a shared commitment within the community to honor the memory of the fallen soldiers. Such acts of generosity and civic-mindedness played a crucial role in the successful realization of community projects during this era.

The acquisition of the lot and the financial support from Crane paved the way for the next phases of the project, including architectural planning, construction and the transformation of the purchased land into a meaningful and lasting memorial space.

A simmering rivalry took shape between the North and Center Villages, injecting a captivating twist into the unfolding community narrative. The heated discourse surrounding the placement of the new town hall cast two formidable figures, Henry W. Cutler of the North Village and Chauncey E. Peck of the Center Village, as central protagonists in this lively and impassioned debate.

Henry W. Cutler, residing in the North Village, was a highly influential and public-spirited individual. Known for his successful grain and milling business, he had already made significant contributions to the community.

One notable example of his generosity later on was the donation of a substantial home to the Town of Wilbraham that later became the town library. This act of philanthropy demonstrated Cutler's commitment to the betterment of the community. The library, dedicated on June 18, 1913, was located on Boston Road between the current fire and police stations. Cutler's influence and contributions marked him as a leading figure in the North Village.

On the other side of the rivalry was Chauncey E. Peck, a prominent figure residing in the Center Village. Peck had established a carriage and wagon manufacturing business located at 380 Main Street in the heart of the town. His influence extended beyond business, as he had served as a representative in the General Court in 1881. Additionally, Peck played a crucial role later on in the erection of the Soldiers Monument in Crane Park and authored the 1913 *History of Wilbraham*. His multifaceted contributions to the town also included serving as town moderator for many years. Notably, Peck was a literary figure, having written and published two well-known poems of local lore, namely "The Parson's Rose" and "Mineola."

The rivalry between the North and Center Villages, fueled by the aspirations of these influential figures, likely added a layer of complexity to the decision-making process. The debate over the location of the new town hall became not just a practical matter but a reflection of the power dynamics and aspirations within the community. The final resolution of this rivalry would undoubtedly shape the town's landscape and contribute to its evolving identity.

The ongoing battle between the North and Center Villages, fueled by the contentious decision regarding the location of the new town hall, took a legal turn when Henry W. Cutler, the prominent figure from the North Village, decided to pursue legal action. In response to the decision on the town hall's location, Cutler, evidently displeased with the outcome, took the initiative to draw up a petition and gather the necessary signatures.

With the petition in hand, Cutler sought to halt the project through legal means. In early January 1886, he took the matter to the state Supreme Court, seeking an injunction to stop the construction of the town hall in its proposed location.

However, the Supreme Court, after careful consideration, chose not to grant the injunction. The court's decision suggested that, in its view, the actions taken by the town in determining the location of the town hall were legal and within the scope of its authority. This legal setback likely frustrated Henry W. Cutler and those who supported his position.

The denial of the injunction allowed the town to proceed with its plans for the town hall in the chosen location, despite the opposition from the North Village and figures like Cutler. The legal dispute, while settled in favor of the town's actions, may have left lingering tensions within the community, reflecting the challenges and conflicts that can arise in the process of decision-making, especially when it comes to matters of public infrastructure and community identity.

The process of awarding the construction bid for the new memorial town hall marked a significant step in moving the project forward. The building committee, responsible for overseeing the construction, initiated the bid request and received three proposals for consideration. On January 21, 1886, the committee convened a meeting to review the bids and make a decision on the contractor for the project. The bids were as follows:

- Chauncey E. Peck: $8,475
- Flynt Building & Construction Company (Palmer): $9,060
- Joseph Hayden (Springfield): highest bid (exact amount not specified)

The committee carefully evaluated the proposals and ultimately selected Chauncey E. Peck as the contractor for the construction of the memorial town hall. Peck's bid, at $8,475, was not only the lowest among the three but also significantly lower than the highest bid, submitted by Joseph Hayden.

This decision likely had a dual impact on the ongoing rivalry between the North and Center Villages. While the selection of Chauncey E. Peck could have been seen as a victory for the Center Village, it might have intensified the dissatisfaction of those in the North Village, particularly considering the earlier legal dispute over the town hall's location.

The awarding of the bid marked a practical and financial milestone for the town hall project. With the contractor in place, the construction phase could commence, bringing the community one step closer to realizing the vision of a central civic space and memorial.

The construction of the Wilbraham Memorial Hall in the unusually mild winter of 1886 marked tangible progress for the project. Despite the typically challenging conditions associated with winter construction, the clement weather allowed for an early start on the building process.

The initial phase involved excavation work for the walls and basement. The foundation of the memorial hall was constructed with brownstone sourced from the abandoned quarry on the west side of West Street

(Stony Hill Road near Manor Road). This local material provided a distinctive and meaningful connection between the building and the town's natural resources. Additionally, the stone used for the portion of the walls above ground level, up to about four feet, was obtained from a quarry in Sixteen Acres.

The decision to use brownstone for the basement walls and locally sourced stone for the above-ground section, combined with the plan to construct the remainder of the building with brick, showcased a thoughtful blend of materials. This approach not only contributed to the structural integrity of the memorial town hall but also incorporated elements that resonated with the town's history and geography.

By April 1886, the construction team had made significant headway, completing the basement section and the wall just above grade. The steady progress indicated the commitment of the community to bring the memorial town hall to fruition. As the building continued to take shape, it became a symbol of civic pride, at least for the Center Village.

The turn of events during the town meeting in April 1886 reflects a significant and unexpected shift in the community's decision regarding the completion of the Wilbraham Memorial Hall. Initially, the town had approved the work that had been done and voted to proceed with the project. However, a change of heart occurred later in the meeting.

As the clock neared 9:00 p.m., some of the voters left the meeting. Subsequently, a motion was made to reconsider completing the project, and surprisingly, this motion passed. The outcome of this reconsideration marked a reversal of the earlier decision, leading to the abandonment of the plan to construct the new memorial town hall.

In the wake of this course correction, the groundwork meticulously set for Memorial Hall found its culmination. This strategic shift seemingly marked an unanticipated conclusion to what had once promised to be a flourishing endeavor. The intricacies of the town's sudden reversal remain cloaked in ambiguity, with historical records providing little insight into the motivations behind this change of heart. However, one could surmise that it was the residents of the North Village who, in their reluctance, steered the community away from witnessing the realization of this project at the town's heart. The foundation that had been laid for the Memorial Hall was eventually filled in.

There is a probability that all the stonework is still intact underground and that the foundation of the memorial town hall may remain as a silent reminder of the unrealized project. The filled foundation, possibly hidden beneath the ground, becomes a poignant symbol of the town's complex history, reflecting both the initial aspirations and the eventual reconsideration that led to the abandonment of the Memorial Hall construction.

The prolonged struggle between the two villages over the construction of the memorial town hall, coupled with the subsequent abandonment of the project, marked a challenging period for the community. As those who initially favored the project eventually gave up, the unresolved issues surrounding the construction led to legal action.

The contractor who had provided the work that was done initiated a lawsuit, likely seeking compensation for the work completed before the project's abandonment. Legal battles of this nature can be protracted and complicated, and in this case, it took about three years for the matter to be settled.

Ultimately, the resolution of the lawsuit came with a financial cost to the town. The expense incurred in settling the matter amounted to a little more than $3,000. While the specific details of the settlement are not available, it is clear that the town had to bear the financial burden resulting from the legal aftermath of the abandoned memorial town hall project.

In a curious turn of events, Chauncey E. Peck erected a residence at 381 Main Street in the year 1888, employing a substantial portion of the timber initially procured for the town hall. It appears that the acquisition of this timber played a pivotal role in his decision, perhaps interpreting the shift in plans for the memorial town hall as a form of settlement for the funds he had invested in the materials, seeing it as a debt duly repaid by the town.

The lack of information about the designer of Memorial Hall in Wilbraham leaves a historical gap, making it challenging to attribute the specific design to an architect. However, the observation that the building looks very similar to the memorial town hall in Monson, designed by George Potter in 1885, raises interesting possibilities.

George E. Potter, an architect with a practice in Springfield, Massachusetts, and later in Hartford, Connecticut, not only designed Monson's memorial town hall, but he was also responsible for designing about twenty-five churches in New England and Long Island.

With the two buildings being constructed around the same time, it's plausible that the same architect, in this case George Potter, might have been involved in the design of both structures. Architects during the late nineteenth century often had distinctive styles, and it was common for them to work on multiple projects in nearby locations.

Both buildings being designed in the High Victorian Gothic style adds further weight to the idea that they could share an architect. High Victorian

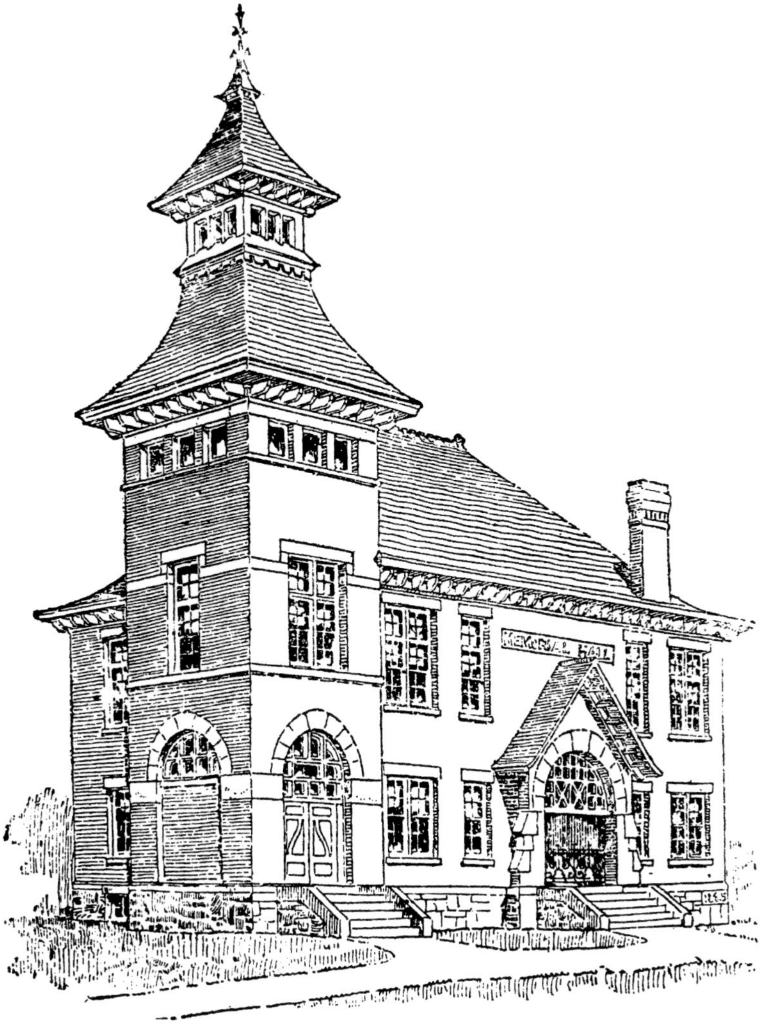

Drawing of the proposed Wilbraham Memorial Hall. *C.E. Peck.*

Gothic was a prevalent architectural style in the late nineteenth century, characterized by intricate details, pointed arches and decorative elements.

While the designer of Wilbraham Memorial Hall remains officially unknown, the architectural similarities and the historical context suggest a potential connection to George Potter.

WHISPERS OF LIBERTY

WILBRAHAM AND HAMPDEN'S CONNECTION TO THE BOSTON TEA PARTY

The Boston Tea Party was not solely a response to a tax on tea but rather was deeply rooted in broader political and economic issues. The Tea Act of 1773, which imposed taxes on tea and granted the East India Company a monopoly on tea sales in the American colonies, was perceived by the colonists as an infringement on their rights and a consolidation of British control.

The protest was fueled by a combination of factors, including the resentment of taxation without representation, the desire to resist perceived overreach of British authority and the economic interests tied to the struggling East India Company. The East India Company was a significant player in English commerce, and the British government sought to rescue it from financial troubles by providing it with a monopoly on tea trade in the American colonies.

The events leading up to the Boston Tea Party culminated on December 16, 1773, when colonists gathered in response to the arrival of a large shipment of tea in Griffin's Wharf, Boston. Governor Thomas Hutchinson insisted that the tea be unloaded and customs duties paid, but the colonists, already agitated, were determined to prevent this. A meeting was convened and a committee formed to approach the governor, and when he failed to provide a satisfactory response by the appointed time, the colonists took matters into their own hands.

On the night of December 16, disguised as Mohawk Indians to conceal their identities, a group of colonists boarded the three tea ships—the *Dartmouth*, the *Eleanor* and the *Beaver*. They proceeded to throw 342 chests of tea into Boston Harbor as a symbolic act of resistance against British policies. This act of protest marked a significant moment in the lead-up to the American Revolution, reflecting the growing tension between the American colonies and the British government over issues of taxation, representation and governance.

One of the participants that night was Robert Sessions, born on March 15, 1752, in Pomfret, Connecticut. His involvement in the act of protest against British taxation was one among the 116 documented participants, a chapter in the larger narrative of colonial resistance. Born in the heart of Connecticut, Sessions found himself entwined with the tumultuous times of the American Revolution.

Beyond his role in the Boston Tea Party, Sessions dedicated himself to the cause of independence by serving in the Revolutionary Army. His commitment and contributions were acknowledged as he ascended to the rank of lieutenant, reflecting the valor and dedication displayed on the battlefield during the struggle for freedom.

Notably, Sessions left behind a valuable account of his experience in the Boston Tea Party. Regrettably, the manuscript detailing his perspective on the events of that night has been lost to the annals of history. However, the dissemination of his account during his time provided valuable insights into the motivations, actions and sentiments of those who participated in the iconic act of defiance.

Robert Sessions was living in Boston at the time with the family of a Mr. Davis, a lumber merchant, and worked as a common laborer. On that fateful evening, as Mr. Davis returned from the town meeting to the humble abode in Boston, a query about the destiny of the tea escaped the lips of a curious Robert Session, who dwelled within his household. "They are now throwing it overboard," came the swift reply. With granted permission, Robert Sessions hastened to the illuminated scene where the orchestrated act of defiance unfolded.

Under the glow of lamps and torches that turned night into day, the wharf stood aglow, revealing every minute detail. A decision was made to be part of the unfolding events, and this common laborer ventured on board, willingly offering his hands for the task at hand. Unlike those who had been appointed to disguise themselves as Mohawk Indians, he was a volunteer—a young man, hailing from Connecticut, within the residence of a lumber merchant in Boston.

While the appointed group, composed largely of Boston's men of family and position, proved insufficient for the swift execution required, other young men joined the effort. The chests of tea were methodically hoisted by a tackle—individuals working in tandem to draw them from the hold, loop ropes around them, and lift them to the deck before ferrying them to the vessel's edge. Systematically, the chests were unsealed, their contents spilled into the harbor and the emptied crates cast overboard. Remarkably, an eerie silence enveloped the wharf despite the presence of numerous onlookers—no clamor, no conversations. It was a meticulous operation focused solely on the tea in the ships' holds.

Upon completing the emptying of the hold, the deck underwent a thorough cleansing. Every item found its designated place, and an onboard officer was summoned to ensure that no harm befell anything other than the targeted tea. The act of defiance, executed with precision and discipline, left the ship bereft of its taxed cargo, marking a pivotal moment in the broader narrative of colonial resistance to British authority.

The composition of the individuals who participated in the Boston Tea Party reflects a diverse cross-section of society during that era. The act of dumping tea into Boston Harbor brought together men from various backgrounds, highlighting a mix of occupations, ethnicities and ages.

About one-third of the participants belonged to skilled artisan professions, such as carpenters, masons and shoemakers. A smaller contingent included individuals from more diverse vocations like merchants, doctors and clerks. However, the majority of those involved were likely apprentices and common laborers, representing a broader spectrum of the working class.

The Tea Party was not confined to a specific ethnic or cultural group; rather, it saw the collaboration of men with diverse origins. Participants included individuals of English, Irish, Scottish, French, African and Portuguese descent. This diversity underscores the widespread discontent with British policies and taxation across various segments of the population.

Additionally, the Boston Tea Party was notably characterized by the involvement of young people. Two-thirds of those with known ages were under twenty, with sixteen teenagers actively participating. Conversely, only a small number, nine individuals, were forty years old or older. This emphasis on youth highlights the energy, passion and fervor of a generation deeply engaged in the revolutionary spirit.

While a significant number of participants hailed from Boston and its vicinity, the Tea Party drew individuals from more distant locations, including Western Massachusetts and other New England colonies. The collective effort to resist British policies united men from different places in a common cause.

The list of named Patriots involved in the Tea Party is a testament to the secrecy surrounding the event. Some participants chose to carry the details of their involvement to their graves, adding an air of mystery to the historical record of this seminal act of defiance.

Robert Sessions's life continued beyond the American Revolutionary War, and he made a significant impact in Western Massachusetts. Settling in what was then Wilbraham and is now Hampden, Sessions became an integral part of the local community. His contributions spanned various roles, showcasing his commitment to public service.

In the postwar era, Sessions served in multiple capacities, reflecting his dedication to the well-being of the town. He held positions such as justice of the peace, town clerk, treasurer and town meeting moderator for Wilbraham. His versatility and active participation in different roles underscored his commitment to the local governance and the community.

The Sessions family continued to be a prominent presence in Wilbraham and Hampden for generations, with succeeding members making substantial contributions to the town and the state of Massachusetts. Their legacy carried forward, with each generation contributing to the growth and development of the community.

The Sessions family home at 300 Wilbraham Road, where Robert Sessions likely played a role in shaping local affairs, stands as a historical testament to their enduring presence in the region. This residence serves as a tangible connection to the past, preserving the memory of a man who played a part in the foundational years of the United States.

Robert Sessions eventually passed away in 1836, leaving behind a legacy of service and community involvement. His final resting place at Old Cemetery in Hampden serves as a marker of the historical significance of his contributions and a reminder of the enduring impact individuals like Sessions had on the shaping of local communities in early America.

The legacy of Robert Sessions, a participant in the Boston Tea Party, was honored and perpetuated through a commendable act of restoration and recognition. Unfortunately, his original marble gravestone, popular in the 1830s, succumbed to the passage of time, crumbling into irreparable pieces. It was in this state that Molly Pruitt, a ninety-three-year-old descendant of Sessions residing in Texas, stepped forward to ensure the preservation of her ancestor's memory.

Motivated by a sense of familial pride and historical reverence, Molly Pruitt funded the replication of Robert Sessions's monument. The new gravestone served as a testament to the enduring connection between

The graves of Robert Sessions and his wife, Anna. *Hampden Historical Commission.*

generations and the commitment to preserving the history of those who contributed to the early shaping of the United States.

The culmination of this effort came to fruition on June 25, 2023, at the Old Hampden Cemetery on Chapin Road. On this day, a grave marker was erected at Robert Sessions's final resting place by the Boston Tea Party Ships & Museum. This act of commemoration acknowledged Sessions's role in the historic events of December 16, 1773.

The installation of the grave marker not only recognized Sessions's contribution to the struggle for American independence but also symbolized the ongoing effort to preserve and honor the legacies of those who played pivotal roles in shaping the nation's history. Molly Pruitt's dedication to this cause ensured that Robert Sessions's memory would endure, so that future generations could reflect on the significance of his actions during a crucial moment in American history.

SOUTH WILBRAHAM MANUFACTURING COMPANY

The history of the town of Wilbraham, with its incorporation in 1763, reflects a rich landscape of industrial development and prominent local families. The division into North and South Parishes in 1782 added an interesting dynamic to the town's growth.

The geographical layout of early manufacturing in Wilbraham was influenced by the presence of waterways. The Scantic River, particularly in the south, played a crucial role in providing power for various manufacturing activities. Lewis Langdon initiated this trend with the establishment of the first sawmill and gristmills along the Scantic River in 1772.

In the northern part of town, Twelve Mile Brook was a significant watercourse, hosting the first mill in the region known as Outward Commons of Springfield or the Mountains. Caleb Stebbins contributed to the industrial landscape by building a gristmill in 1762 along Twelve Mile Brook. These smaller waterways proved more convenient for harnessing power compared to the larger Chicopee River, where more extensive manufacturing emerged in the mid- to late 1800s.

The woolen mill built in 1843 by Deacon Sumner Sessions stands out as a notable manufacturing establishment along the Scantic River. Located at what is now 498 Main Street in Hampden, this mill held the distinction of being the largest mill in the area. The granite walls of the mill were sourced from nearby hills on Chapin Road, quarried by the Flynt Granite Company of Monson.

An intriguing historical connection is revealed through Deacon Sumner Sessions, who was a descendant of Robert Sessions. Robert Sessions participated in the Boston Tea Party and settled in Wilbraham in 1781. The Sessions family, with their roots in the area, played a significant role in the town's development, and their prominence is evident in the local history.

This snapshot of Wilbraham's industrial and familial history provides a glimpse into the town's evolution, highlighting the impact of waterways, the growth of manufacturing and the enduring influence of families like the Sessionses.

This historical account further unfolds with the mill rented out to Levi Bradford and Eleazer Scripter in 1844, equipped with a single set of machinery. Under their management, the mill successfully produced high-quality satinets. However, Levi Bradford retired in 1847, prompting a transition in the mill's ownership and operations.

In that same year, the mill came under the management of Luther E. Sage, William V. Sessions and Samuel Beebe, who formed a partnership. This trio took charge of the mill, marking a new phase in its history. Subsequently, this partnership was succeeded by the firm of Scripter, Sage and Company.

Under the leadership of Scripter, Sage and Company, the mill experienced notable growth and diversification. The production capacity of the works was expanded, and the range of manufactured goods broadened. In addition to satinets, the mill began producing tweeds, cassimere and doeskins, showcasing a strategic response to market demands and an expansion of the mill's product offerings. This evolution in ownership and management reflects the adaptive nature of the mill's operators, who not only sustained its operations but also enhanced its productivity and product variety.

In 1856, a significant development occurred in the history of the mill when a new company was formed, leading to a change in its name to the South Wilbraham Manufacturing Company. This transformation was accompanied by the incorporation of the company with a substantial capital of $200,000, indicating a commitment to further expansion and development.

The company's commitment to growth was evident in 1862 when a large addition was made to the mill, accompanied by the installation of new machinery. This investment in infrastructure and technology likely aimed to enhance the mill's production capabilities and overall efficiency.

According to Rufus P. Stebbins's account in the 1864 *History of Wilbraham*, the South Wilbraham Manufacturing Company proved to be a highly successful business during this period. Stebbins notes that in 1863, the company achieved a significant production milestone by turning out one thousand yards of satinet daily. This production volume underscored the mill's efficiency and productivity, contributing to its success in the local and potentially broader markets.

This mention of the mill's success and high production output in the historical record provides a glimpse into the economic prosperity and industrial prowess of the South Wilbraham Manufacturing Company during the mid-nineteenth century.

After changes in ownership, the mill was transformed into the Lacowsic Woolen Company under the management of Charles Parsons. While the business began operations with promise, Parsons ultimately faced challenges that led to its failure. Subsequently, the reins of the Lacowsic Woolen Company were taken up by Brown & Chapman. However, the specifics of this transition and the subsequent operations are not well known.

Later on, Hinsdale Smith assumed control of the mill, with his son actively involved in its management. Under the Smith family's leadership, the Lacowsic Woolen Company flourished, boasting five sets of machinery and sixteen looms. The workforce comprised seventy-five to eighty employees, reflecting a substantial labor force for the time.

The mill, under the Smiths, specialized in the production of fancy cassimeris. Monthly output reached an impressive sixteen thousand yards, indicating a robust manufacturing operation. The mention of "fancy cashmere" shows a focus on producing high-quality, patterned woolen fabrics, possibly catering to a niche market or satisfying specific fashion trends of the period.

The Lacowsic Woolen Company's ability to adapt to changes in ownership and management, coupled with its success in producing a popular and sought-after fabric, demonstrates the resilience and versatility of the mill as it continued to play a significant role in the local industrial landscape.

This history adds an interesting layer to the operations of the Lacowsic Woolen Company, emphasizing the company's significant presence in the community. The ownership of numerous homes and barns by the mill owners in the vicinity of the mill complex was a testament to the company's influence on the local community.

One notable property was a house directly across the street from the mill, originally owned by Robert A. Sessions. In 1848, Sessions sold this house to the owners of the woolen mill, solidifying a connection between the residential and industrial aspects of the community. The house and its accompanying barn played crucial roles in the mill's operations.

The house earned the name "Soap House," a reference to a specific function within the manufacturing process. The product produced in this house was used for washing the wool processed in the mill. The Soap House played a vital role in preparing the raw materials for the woolen manufacturing operations, contributing to the overall efficiency of the mill.

The barn associated with the Soap House had a practical purpose as well: it served as a storage facility for the wool. This underscores the interconnectedness of various structures in the mill complex, each playing a specific role in the production process.

Before the mill's ownership, the historical record notes that the Soap House was used for the manufacture of soft soap. This highlights the adaptive nature of the building, repurposed to suit different industrial needs over time.

The original three-story building, with the unique feature of its first story being entirely constructed of granite, stands as a testament to the durability and robustness of the early industrial structures. This building likely housed the primary manufacturing operations and machinery.

Another significant structure within the mill complex is a three-story granite building with a smokestack located near the river. This building served as additional manufacturing space and housed equipment related to the processing or finishing of woolen goods.

In 1862, an expansion took place with the construction of a one-story "weaving room" addition to the east side of the two-story building. This addition accommodated looms and weaving equipment, playing a crucial role in the production process. The expansion in 1862 reflected a period of growth and increased capacity for the mill.

The "Soap House." *Hampden Historical Commission.*

The dam near the three-story granite building shows the reliance on water power for its operations. This dam, strategically located on the river, would have harnessed the energy from the flowing water to drive machinery within the mill complex. The use of water power was a common practice in early industrial settings, providing a sustainable and efficient source of energy.

Additionally, there was another older dam farther upstream, just west of the Chapin Road Bridge. In 1847, a significant development occurred when Erasmus Chaffee deeded the right to construct a canal across his property to Samuel Beebe, William V. Sessions, Eleazer Scripter and Luther Sage. This canal was designed to be four feet wide at the bottom and eight feet wide in the clear on top of the water. The purpose of this canal was to carry water to the Scripter, Sage and Company mill, providing additional water power to drive the mill's machinery.

The canal followed a path across higher ground, alongside the original road, and entered a penstock supported by granite piers near the millpond. This engineering feat allowed for the efficient transportation of water to power the mill. The canal and penstock system illustrates the innovative approaches taken by mill owners to secure a reliable and controlled water source for industrial operations.

It was said that "boys" would take shelter under the penstock while fishing. This would reflect the way in which the infrastructure of the mill, beyond its industrial purposes, became a part of the community's everyday life and recreational activities. Such stories contribute to the local history, providing a glimpse into the lives of individuals living in proximity to the mill complex.

As the mill complex stood stoically along the river, its millpond, a shimmering expanse of water, took on a dual role in the lives of local residents. In the summertime, when the air was warm and inviting, the millpond transformed into a haven of leisure and recreation for the community.

The pond, encircled by the granite walls of the mill, became a natural gathering place. Local residents sought respite from the summer heat by diving off a large boulder that stood sentinel at the water's edge. Laughter echoed as children leaped into the refreshing embrace of the pond, creating timeless memories that would be cherished for generations. Fishing lines dangled from the hands of hopeful anglers, casting out into the calm waters to lure in the elusive catch of the day. The millpond, with its serene beauty, became a tranquil retreat for those seeking the simple joys of a lazy afternoon spent by the water's edge.

As winter cast its icy spell, the millpond underwent a magical transformation. The stillness of the water gave way to a frozen expanse that beckoned both young and old. In the heart of winter, the millpond became a natural ice rink, its surface transformed into a glistening sheet of frozen delight. Local children, bundled up against the winter chill, skated across the frozen pond, their laughter harmonizing with the crisp winter air. A large boulder, once a launching pad for summer divers, now stood as a stoic sentinel on the frozen stage, witnessing the joyous ballet of ice skaters.

The community embraced the winter wonderland with open arms. It was said that the ice thickness reached an impressive eighteen inches or more, rendering the frozen pond safe for skating from mid-November through mid-March. In January, a new ritual unfolded as the men of the town took to the ice with hand tools, cutting and harvesting the frozen bounty.

This carefully collected ice was destined for the icehouse, a structure that held the promise of cool relief in the warmer months. The hard work of cutting and storing ice in the heart of winter translated into the luxury of refrigeration during the sweltering summer days. The millpond, a year-round companion to the community, not only bore witness to the ebb and flow of seasons but also became an integral part of the shared stories and traditions that defined life in the shadow of the mill complex.

A snippet from the 1879 newspaper offers a brief but intriguing glimpse into the history of the Lacowsic Mill and the dynamics of industrial labor during that period. The mention of a strike suggests a period of labor unrest within the Lacowsic Mill. Strikes were not uncommon in the nineteenth century, as workers often organized to protest poor working conditions, low wages or other grievances. The term *tramps* would refer to itinerant workers or laborers moving from place to place in search of employment.

The resolution of the strike, indicated by the phrase "the strike in the mill is over," suggests that the management and labor force reached an agreement or settlement. The departure of "most of the tramps" would signify that individuals not directly associated with the local workforce or community moved on once the strike concluded.

The mention of the local workforce returning, expressed as "the help hereabouts have gone back," indicates a sense of normalcy returning to the community. The resolution of the strike had a local impact, influencing not only the mill but also the broader community and economy.

Postcard of the mill ruins. *Digital Commonwealth.*

While the snippet is brief, it speaks volumes about the social and economic dynamics of the time. Labor relations, strikes and the movement of workers were integral aspects of the evolving industrial landscape during the late nineteenth century.

The fiery demise of the Lacowsic Mill in 1892 marked the end of an era for the industrial complex. The loss was significant, and the decision not to rebuild spoke to a combination of economic factors and the shifting landscape of industrial logistics.

The proposed railroad of 1870, a potential lifeline for the mill's operations, failed to materialize. Without the efficient transportation that a railroad could have provided, the cost of importing raw materials and exporting finished goods likely became a significant financial burden. Mills in other communities with railroad access enjoyed a competitive advantage in terms of transportation costs, making them more economically viable.

The charred remnants of the Lacowsic Mill's granite walls stood as solemn sentinels, bearing witness to the vibrant industrial past that once thrived on the banks of the river. These enduring walls, though scarred by the flames, held within them the echoes of an era when the mill hummed with the rhythms of production and community life.

Decades later, in 1968, the final chapter of the Lacowsic Mill's physical legacy unfolded. The remaining stones, survivors of the fire and the passage of time, found a new purpose in the widening of Main Street near the bend of the river. The repurposing of these stones became a tangible link to the past, connecting the modern landscape with the industrial history that had shaped the community.

The Lacowsic Mill, once a bustling center of industry, became a chapter in Wilbraham and Hampden town history that faded away, leaving behind the enduring memory of its granite walls and its stories. The rise and fall of the mill mirrored the broader narrative of industrialization, transportation challenges and the ebb and flow of economic fortunes in nineteenth and early twentieth-century America.

THE RANDOLPH BEEBE HOUSE, ITS RATTLESNAKE AND THE LEGEND OF THE WHIPPOORWILL

In the peaceful town of Wilbraham, nestled along the picturesque East Road (Beebe Road), a historic house stands as a silent witness to the tales of the past. Built around 1785, this residence has seen the passage of time and generations, each leaving behind a piece of history. One such captivating story revolves around the earlier occupants, the Mack family.

Daniel Chappel, the original owner, did not linger in this charming abode for long. The house soon found itself a new set of inhabitants: Nathan and Mary Mack, who settled in around 1790. Little did they know that their family would be forever linked to a curious and heart-pounding episode that unfolded on the grounds of this historic dwelling.

Around 1810, Mary Mack, the resilient matriarch, witnessed an extraordinary event that etched itself into local folklore. One day, as Mary glanced out the door, she spotted her daughter seated in the lush grass, engrossed in play. Intrigued, Mary approached quietly, only to discover a scene that would send shivers down her spine.

To her astonishment, nestled in her daughter's lap was a large rattlesnake, coiled and seemingly undisturbed. Maintaining her composure, Mary swiftly retreated to the house. Determined to protect her child, she grabbed a small tub and hurried back to the scene.

With nerves of steel, Mary dropped the tub over the unsuspecting snake as it slithered away from her daughter. Swiftly pulling her child to safety, Mary wasted no time in returning to the safety of their home. The dramatic events, however, were far from over.

Upon Nathan's return from his daily endeavors, he noticed the inconspicuous tub in the yard. Unaware of the serpent concealed within, he picked it up. Suddenly, with a burst of energy, the rattlesnake sprang forth, revealing itself. Thinking on his feet, Nathan swiftly wielded his hoe and brought an end to the dangerous intruder.

In a strange turn of events, Nathan decided to commemorate the incident by removing the rattles from the snake. These rattles, once symbols of danger, were transformed into an unusual family heirloom. Nathan presented them to his daughter, who, in turn, preserved the keepsake for several generations, passing down not just a house but a tale of courage and quick thinking.

The house at 48 Beebe Road, Wilbraham, continues to stand as a silent testament to the lives lived within its walls. The Mack family's encounter with a rattlesnake, though perilous at the time, became an indelible part of the home's rich history, weaving together the threads of ordinary moments that, over time, transform into extraordinary stories.

This old house had witnessed generations come and go, each leaving behind a chapter in its storied history. By the time the lens captured its image in the sepia tones of 1913, it was under the ownership of Randolph Beebe. However, the house's tale stretches further back, entwined with the legacy of Thomas Gilligan, Randolph's father-in-law, who had held its keys since the 1860s.

Randolph Beebe, a figure whose life echoed through the halls of the historic abode, became the custodian of its memories. Little did he know that this house, steeped in the echoes of time, would play an unexpected role in shaping American literature.

48 Beebe Road, 1913. *C.E. Peck.*

In the aftermath of Randolph Beebe's passing in 1923, the house fell into a state of vacancy. An eerie quiet settled on the property as it stood dormant, weathering the passage of seasons. However, it was during this seemingly uneventful period that the house embarked on an unintentional journey into the realm of literature.

Word began to circulate about the house at 48 Beebe Road, whispered tales that hinted at something extraordinary. As fate would have it, a curious writer stumbled upon this vacant abode, drawn by the mystique that seemed to cling to its weathered façade.

The author, captivated by the charm and aura of the empty residence, found inspiration in its silent halls and forgotten rooms. The house became a canvas for the writer's imagination, a backdrop against which a tale unfolded. The creaking floorboards and the faded wallpaper whispered stories of bygone days, weaving themselves into the fabric of the narrative.

In this unexpected manner, the house became an unsung muse, contributing its essence to the world of American literature. The vacant dwelling, once filled with the warmth of family life, now echoed with the voices of characters born from the imagination of a writer who saw in its emptiness a canvas waiting to be painted with words.

The house, having served as an unwitting inspiration, remained a silent spectator to its newfound literary legacy. As the years passed, its walls held within them not just the echoes of its own past but also the whispers of a story that had transcended the boundaries of time and imagination—a tale that unfolded during the quiet interlude when the house, empty yet full of history, left its mark on the literary landscape.

The summer of 1928 found the renowned horror and science fiction writer H.P. Lovecraft embarking on a tour through the enchanting landscapes of New England. One stop on his itinerary was an eight-day sojourn at the residence of Evanore Beebe, a gracious host who welcomed Lovecraft into her home, Maplehurst. This abode stood proudly a short distance from the Beebe Road home at 782 Monson Road.

During his stay at Maplehurst, Lovecraft found himself immersed in the mystique of New England folklore. It was amid the verdant surroundings and the whispers of the countryside that he encountered a tale that would weave its way into the fabric of one of his most famous short stories, "The Dunwich Horror."

Lovecraft, always attuned to the eerie and the supernatural, learned of an old New England legend shared by the locals. The tale spoke of whippoorwill birds as ominous omens of death, believed to have the power to capture departing souls. This unsettling narrative took root in Lovecraft's imagination, and he drew inspiration from it for his literary creation.

However, in a twist of fate, Lovecraft attributed the origin of this legend to the house on Beebe Road, formerly owned by Randolph Beebe. In a letter written in 1934, Lovecraft reflected on his experiences, stating, "I saw the ruinous, deserted old Randolph Beebe house where the whippoorwills cluster abnormally." This revelation marked the genesis of the legend that would become an integral part of "The Dunwich Horror."

Thus, the house at 48 Beebe Road, steeped in its own history and adorned with the lore of whippoorwill omens, unknowingly contributed to the rich tapestry of Lovecraft's literary legacy. Its silent walls, once witness to the passage of time and the story of a rattlesnake, now became part of a narrative that transcended reality, lingering in the dark corners of the horror genre for years to come. The convergence of Lovecraft's visit, the Beebe family homes and the whispers of New England legends wove a tale that blurred the lines between fiction and the mystique of the region's haunting folklore.

PRESERVING HISTORY

THE REMARKABLE RESCUE OF SOUTH WILBRAHAM'S JONAH BEEBE HOUSE

In the quaint town of South Wilbraham, nestled in the heart of the newly formed South Parish, there lived a man named Jonah Beebe. Born on April 14, 1750, in East Haddam, Connecticut Colony, Jonah's life unfolded against the backdrop of British colonial America.

In the spring of 1772, Jonah exchanged vows with Ruth Dowley in the charming town of Lyme, Connecticut Colony. United in matrimony on the same month and day as Jonah's birth, the couple embarked on a journey that would lead them to the picturesque landscapes of South Wilbraham.

Yearning for a place to call home, Jonah and Ruth built a splendid Federal residence in 1783 on Third Road, now known as 421 Glendale Road in Hampden. Their abode became a haven where they raised at least six sons and two daughters, creating a bustling and lively household.

The Beebe family's influence extended beyond their home, as Jonah was not only a loving father but also a community builder. Recognizing the importance of education, Jonah took it upon himself to construct a schoolhouse just down the road from their residence, now standing at 320 Glendale Road, Hampden. The echoes of children's laughter and the rustling of pages in that humble schoolhouse became a testament to Jonah's commitment to knowledge and community.

As the years passed, the Beebe family became integral to the fabric of South Wilbraham. Jonah's dedication to his family and community was evident in the legacy he left behind. However, life's journey comes with its inevitable conclusion. On March 25, 1831, Jonah Beebe breathed his last breath at the age of eighty. His final resting place was marked in the South Wilbraham Cemetery, now known as the Old Hampden Cemetery on Chapin Road. The community mourned the loss of a patriarch, but Jonah's spirit endured in the stories told around the hearths of South Wilbraham.

In 1795, the property changed hands as Steven Newell and his wife, Louisa Sikes, took ownership. Little did they know that their story would become an indelible thread in the fabric of South Wilbraham's narrative as well.

Steven Newell, born on June 7, 1758, was not just a homeowner but a living embodiment of resilience and commitment to his family and country. His roots traced back to Dudley, Massachusetts, and his father, Abijah Newell, born on January 9, 1731, moved to the Wilbraham area in 1775.

The looming specter of the Revolutionary War cast its shadow over the Newell family. Abijah, with a staggering eleven children, found himself unable to serve. In a gesture that spoke volumes about familial bonds and patriotism, he offered his son Steven as a replacement. Steven, born on the precipice of a nation's struggle for independence on June 7, 1758, stepped into his father's shoes with courage and a sense of duty.

Steven Newell's military service was marked by unwavering dedication. Drafted into the Revolutionary War, he served "faithfully and with courage." His deployment included a stint at the pivotal Fort Ticonderoga in New York, where he stood tall from March 1 to April 11, 1777. The echoes of battles and the camaraderie of fellow Patriots must have left an indelible mark on his spirit.

But Steven's commitment did not waver with the passing of time. In 1780, he enlisted once again, dedicating five more months to the cause that had become the crucible of a burgeoning nation. Not just a soldier, Steven also served as a fifer, adding a musical note to the harsh realities of war.

As the Revolutionary War drew to a close, Steven returned to civilian life, bringing with him the experiences and stories that would become part of the lore passed down through generations. In 1795, he and Louisa embarked on a new chapter as they acquired the property in South Wilbraham.

The Newell homestead once again became a haven for family life. Ten children filled its rooms with laughter and footsteps, each contributing to the legacy that began with Steven's brave service and continued through the generations. The Newell name, etched in history, stood as a testament to the enduring spirit of those who weathered the storms of revolution to build a foundation for the future in the quiet landscapes of South Wilbraham.

The Newell homestead continued its journey through time, passing from generation to generation, each chapter adding new dimensions to its storied history. John Newell, the sixth child of Steven and Louisa, emerged as the custodian of the family legacy. Born on May 10, 1792, John and his wife, Pauline Sophronia Bigelow, became the third stewards of this historical residence.

John and Pauline's union was blessed with eleven children, filling the halls of the homestead with the exuberance of a growing family. John's commitment to community and public service also manifested itself beyond the walls of their home. In 1841, he ascended to the Massachusetts Senate and House of Representatives, leaving an indelible mark on the political landscape.

The passing years saw the Newell homestead witness the ebb and flow of life, and on January 3, 1875, John Newell departed this world at the age of eighty-two. His contributions to both family and community lingered in the air of South Wilbraham, shaping the legacy of the Newell name.

With John's passing, the homestead found itself in the hands of the next in line, as his son Alonzo B. Newell stepped forward as the fourth owner and third generation to farm the land. Under Alonzo's care, the property continued to be a symbol of continuity and familial dedication.

As fate would have it, on March 28, 1878, a significant moment unfolded in the history of the region. The South Parish of Wilbraham completed its transformation, leading to the creation of the town of Hampden. The Newells, now residents of Hampden, retained their ancestral property as it stood witness to the changing tides of administrative divisions.

The Newell family lovingly nurtured and cultivated the land until 1923, when a new chapter began. The property then passed into the hands of the Gerrish family, who became its devoted custodians. For nearly a century, the Gerrish family preserved the homestead's historical charm, maintaining its legacy until 2016. Like their predecessors, they were deeply involved in the community, serving as pillars of strength and continuity.

Through wars, political changes and the evolution of towns, the Beebes, Newells and Gerrishes and their homestead stood as anchors, connecting the past to the present. The threads of its history, woven with tales of service, family and community, created a tapestry that endured across generations and ownerships. As the Gerrish family maintained the property into the twenty-first century, they became the stewards of a living testament to the rich heritage that began with Jonah Beebe and continued through the Newell family in the quiet town of Hampden.

The tale of this homestead takes an unexpected turn, one that resonates with the struggles faced by many historic homes in the face of modern

Jonah Beebe's Home was built in 1783. *Hampden Historical Commission.*

development. In 2016, the property changed hands once again, falling into the possession of a developer with plans to demolish the venerable homestead and make way for new constructions. It was a fate all too familiar for many historic homes across the country.

Yet this particular story takes a heartening twist. In a stroke of fortune, the historic home found saviors in the form of Randy and Kim, friends with a deep appreciation for the past. With the home facing the looming threat of a wrecking ball, Randy and Kim took on the formidable challenge of preserving the rich history embedded within the walls of this historic site.

Their commitment to conservation and historical preservation shone through as they embarked on a painstaking journey of restoration. Every creaky floorboard, every weathered beam and every historical detail, including the many fireplaces with a very large center chimney, was given the attention it deserved. The result of their dedication is a testament to the enduring beauty of historic architecture and the power of passionate individuals to rewrite the fate of a piece of living history.

Today, as you step onto the property, you are greeted not by the rumble of construction machinery but by the echoes of centuries past, seamlessly blended with the modern comforts of Randy and Kim's lovingly restored home. The historic homestead, once on the brink of demolition, now stands tall, a living monument to the resilience of history and the transformative impact of those who choose to preserve it.

Randy and Kim's efforts saved not only a house but also a piece of the community's soul. Their commitment to the preservation of the historic homestead ensures that future generations can continue to marvel at the craftsmanship and stories that have unfolded within its walls over the centuries. It stands as a beacon of hope and a reminder that, even in the face of progress, the echoes of the past can endure with the right stewards at the helm.

Randy's recounting of a pivotal moment during the restoration of the Newell homestead adds a touch of serendipity to the tale. The challenges of restoring an abandoned, centuries-old home weighed heavily on Randy and Kim, particularly when faced with a damp and dimly lit cellar. As the daunting reality of the undertaking settled in, Randy couldn't help but wonder about the enormity of the task.

In the midst of this uncertainty, a small beam of light broke through the darkness, quite literally and metaphorically. Randy's attention was drawn to a horseshoe on the wall, a symbol steeped in folklore and superstition. According to legend, an upside-down horseshoe signifies that luck is spilling out. In a spontaneous gesture, Randy reached up and turned the horseshoe right-side up, an act that would prove to be more than symbolic.

At that very moment, as if touched by a stroke of fortune, Randy's son excitedly shouted from another part of the house, "Hey Dad, I just found a bag of silver coins dating back to the mid-1800s!" The synchronicity of the horseshoe's reversal and the discovery of the coins became a turning point in the restoration journey.

Randy's sprinting ascent from the cellar to the upper floors encapsulated the exhilaration of a moment where fortune smiles on the restoration endeavor. From that day forward, with the horseshoe now upright, the Newell homestead seemed to embrace a renewed sense of luck and prosperity. Randy and Kim, spurred by this stroke of serendipity, continued their meticulous restoration work on the property, breathing life back into the timeworn walls of the historic home.

The horseshoe, once a silent witness to centuries of history, became a symbol not only of superstition but also of resilience and good fortune. As Randy and Kim look back on the journey that brought the homestead from the brink of demolition to its present glory, they can't help but reflect on the fortuitous moment in the dimly lit cellar—a moment that not only saved a bag of silver coins but also preserved a piece of history for generations to come.

The successful preservation of the Newell homestead stands as a testament to the power of community, tenacious individuals and a shared passion for safeguarding history. The tireless efforts of Will D'Angelo from the Hampden Historical Commission played a pivotal role in this journey. Their relentless advocacy and persistence in communicating with the developer became the driving force that eventually compelled the developer to reconsider their plans. At one point, when the house was on the verge of demolition, Will was prepared to handcuff himself to a post inside the home using historical handcuffs that once belonged to Arthur H. Gerrish, a former town constable who had once lived in the home. He felt this act would be a fitting tribute to save this historic home.

The collaborative spirit extended beyond the local level, as Congressman Richard Neal and his office lent their support to the cause. Preservation Massachusetts, represented by Stacia Caplanson, brought expertise and advocacy to the table. The Hampden Board of Selectmen, led by Pamela Courtney, played a crucial role in local governance, ensuring that the importance of preserving historical landmarks was recognized.

The Hampden Historical Society, along with Linda Krawiec, Arthur A. Booth from the Hampden VFW and Tyler S. Witkop, the editor of the *Hampden/Wilbraham Times*, all contributed their voices to the collective call for preservation. The Hampden Library, Sergeant Mike Cooney of the Hampden Police Department and Jonah Keane from the Mass Audubon Society Laughing Brook Wildlife Sanctuary were among the many others who joined the effort.

This collaborative initiative brought together various stakeholders, each contributing in their own way to ensure the survival of a piece of local history. The acknowledgment of these individuals and organizations underscores the importance of community engagement in safeguarding the cultural heritage that shapes our shared identity.

The story of the Beebe homestead's preservation found its way into the pages of *Living Spaces* magazine, further highlighting the significance of this achievement. Randy and Kim's restoration efforts, fueled by community support and advocacy, transformed the property into a living testament to the power of collective action and the enduring value of preserving our historical treasures. The Newell homestead, once on the brink of destruction, now stands proudly as a symbol of resilience, community and the enduring legacy of those who fought to save it from the hands of the wrecking ball.

EARLY LIFE ON SPRINGFIELD MOUNTAIN, 1730–1750

The early settlers of these "Outward Commons" or "Springfield Mountain," now the towns of Wilbraham, Hampden and Ludlow, were very hardy and adventurous individuals. Those early times were not easy for them. They struggled with the stubborn soil and other difficulties that go along with living in the wilderness.

Many of these first settlers bought land from the original proprietors who received these land grants on February 3, 1685, which they never settled. In 1674, William Pynchon, Elizur Holyoke and others purchased the Outward Commons from the Native Americans. This became part of the town of Springfield. In 1636, Pynchon received the deed, giving him title to most of what is now Springfield, West Springfield, Chicopee, Longmeadow and Agawam. In exchange, he paid the local Agawam Indians eighteen fathoms of wampum, eighteen coats and several hoes, hatchets and knives.

In 1684, there was a threat that Sir Edmund Andros, governor of Massachusetts, would take away the colony's charter, causing all the unappropriated lands, the Outward Commons, to revert to the Crown, becoming the property of the king of England. For this reason, land grants were given out in 1685.

This land was abundant with deer, wild turkeys, squirrels, beavers, muskrats, minks, foxes and other wildlife. The rivers and streams were no different, as trout, pickerel and salmon, weighing from seven to twelve pounds, could be found. Bears were not as expected, and "wildcats" had bounties issued by the Town of Springfield for their destruction.

Nathaniel Hitchcock was the first person to come out to the Outward Commons in the summer of 1730, from the settlement of Springfield, which was on the banks of the Great River, Connecticut River. He cleared and broke the ground of two acres and erected a log hut on the west side of West Road, now 603 Main Street, Wilbraham. After planting his two acres of wheat, Hitchcock returned to his home at the Springfield settlement to spend the winter.

In May 1731, Hitchcock returned with his wife, Hannah Taylor, whom he married the previous year, and their four-month-old daughter, Hannah. From this point forward, they all took up residence in this wilderness year-round. They also had four more children afterward: Nathaniel, Mary, Gideon and Silas. Their closest neighbors would be nine miles away at the Springfield settlement. During his first year, Hitchcock was exceptionally industrious, tending to his crops and fields with diligence. He planted corn, gathered wheat, mowed grass, dried and stacked hay and husked and stored corn. In the winter, he found comfort in the melodies of his wife's singing and the joyful laughter of his children, which provided a warm respite from his hard work.

The following spring, the robins and bluebirds returned, but better than that, Noah Alvord and his wife, Hannah Burt, along with their two children, Hannah and Moses, took up residence just six hundred feet south of their homestead on the east side of the West Road, now 648 Main Street, Wilbraham. The couple had two other children afterward, Aaron and Elizabeth.

The Hitchcocks and the Alvords became very close and relied on each other to survive hardships. That first year, Nathaniel helped Noah clear his land and build his house. In return, Noah helped Nathaniel with his work. The two wives also helped each other out with family needs. They were inseparable.

Word got out to the Springfield settlement that the land was good and that conditions were favorable for establishing a prosperous farm. The two families who had already established their homestead on Springfield Mountain were doing very well and were very happy.

In the next year, 1733, Daniel Warner and Sergeant Moses Burt came out to join the other two families in making this place their home. Daniel Warner brought out his wife, Jerusha Hitchcock, and soon after had their first child, named Comfort. She was the first child born on Springfield Mountain. The Warners would have an additional seven children. They settled on the east side of West Road, 576 Main Street, about 1,100 feet north of Nathaniel

Hitchcock's place. Sergeant Moses Burt brought out his newly married wife, Hannah Warriner, and they eventually had four children: Hannah, Eunice, Moses and Lovice. This family settled on the west side of West Road, 651 Main Street, approximately 950 feet south of Nathaniel Hitchcock's place.

In 1734, Nathaniel Warriner and his wife, Margaret Merrick Warriner, moved out to West Road, 599 Main Street. Their residence was just to the north, next door to the Hitchcocks. Nathaniel and Margaret never had any children. Nathaniel was a very prominent citizen—the donor to the ministry and school fund upon his death in 1780 at the age of seventy-seven. As early as 1737, education for the children of this new land was very important to the settlers. The Town of Springfield appropriated three pounds for the support of a school.

Besides the Burt family, of the five original settlers, no descendants remained in town in 1863. Soon after, other settlers started to put down roots in this area. Within the first ten years after Nathaniel Hitchcock, there was Thomas Glover, Samuel Warner, Samuel Stebbins, David Merrick, John Jones, David Jones, Abel Bliss, Daniel Lamb, Thomas Merrick, David Warriner, Isaac Brewer, David Chapin, Moses Bartlett and Nathaniel Bliss. There were a few more families who settled here around 1741. That year, Stephen Stebbins was the first to settle in the south part of the mountains, which is Hampden today. He came from the Longmeadow section of Springfield and settled on the north bank of the Scantic River on the West Road. Aaron Stebbins, his brother, built just north of his home. Lewis Langdon settled on the corner between them and built the first sawmill in the Outward Commons or Springfield Mountain.

As mentioned previously, in 1733, the first child born in the Outward Commons was Comfort, daughter of Daniel and Jerusha Warner. The first person to die was David Jones on August 19, 1736. He was the son of David and Hannah "Stiles" Jones. It was said that the father did not want his child to be the first tenant of the burying ground at Adams Cemetery, so they buried their son at the old Springfield Cemetery. Two other deaths occurred before 1741, and both were also interred in Springfield.

The first tenant of the burying ground at Adams Cemetery was thirty-nine-year-old Elizabeth Cockril, who died on April 26, 1741. Elizabeth, a widow from Boston, was on a visit to her sister, Samuel Warner's wife, and became ill and died. Mr. Warner buried her here, and even though he was not a stonecutter, he found two flat stones and engraved her name and the date of her death—that was the first grave located in that cemetery. Her stones are located in the southeast quarter of the old section. The next burials seemingly were three young children of Daniel Warner in 1746, 1748 and 1749. These graves are marked by a single stone.

By 1741, there were twenty-four to twenty-six families living in the Outward Commons. Most of their homes were framed, with the sawmill in Sixteen Acres supplying the cut lumber. This was the closest sawmill at the time until other sawmills were built on Twelve Mile Brook and the Scantic River. These early houses were poorly finished, with scantily glazed windows and meager furnishings. Many of the interior walls in these homes were partially plastered. As time went on, the early settlers improved their homes and even replaced them with homes of finer quality.

From the higher elevations of the Outward Commons, the settlers could gaze westward across the unbroken forest, swamps, ponds and meadows to see the smoke rising from the homes of friendly settlers on the banks of the Great River, Connecticut River. This is the place where their meeting house was located, nine miles away. It was still a long journey to Sunday worship.

These new settlers were very religious, and a petition was drawn up to have the Outward Commons become its very own precinct of Springfield. On January 6, 1741, Jonathan Belcher, governor of Massachusetts Bay, approved the "Outward Commons on the east side of the Great River," or "Mountains of Springfield," to become the Fourth Precinct of Springfield.

On March 12, 1741, a meeting was held at David Mirick's house. William Pynchon was the moderator. David Mirick was chosen as clerk, and Thomas Mirick, Isaac Brewer and Nathaniel Warriner were chosen as the Precinct Committee. Isaac Brewer became treasurer; David Mirick, Thomas Mirick and Samuel Stebbins became assessors; and Nathaniel Warriner became collector.

The first precinct meeting was held on March 25, 1741, at the home of Isaac Brewer. One of the orders of business was to see whether they would give the worthy Mr. Noah Mirrick a call to see if he would be interested in being the minister of the newly formed precinct of the Outward Commons. They also took advice from the three neighboring ministers. On April 17, without waiting for the advice of the three neighboring ministers, they unanimously voted to call Noah Mirick and offer him the ministry of the Outward Commons.

On May 26, 1741, Noah Mirick accepted the ministry and settled among them. The salary was worked out along with giving the deed for the overplus land of the second division to him. In addition to all of this, it was agreed to build the minister's house at the location for him to determine.

Reverend Noah Merrick assumed his official role as the first minister on June 24, 1741, the same day the church was organized. The ordaining council was to have taken place under a large oak tree in the yard of Daniel Warner's house (area of 576 Main Street). On this morning, a crude pulpit of rough boards was constructed, and a few seats of boards and logs were arranged around it to accommodate the people. Unfortunately, the weather was not clear. As the morning gave way to afternoon, the weather became severe with an approaching storm. As the rain started, the people hurriedly adjourned the service to Nathaniel Warriner's barn (599 Main Street). The ordination services were continued there.

On November 6, 1741, a vote was taken to build a pound in the precinct, at the charge of the precinct, so that any stray cattle or other livestock could be housed to avoid destruction of settler property. It is believed that this pound was in the area of what is Faculty Street today.

At a meeting held on May 4, 1742, a vote was made to build Reverend Noah Merrick's house on Wigwam Hill, part of the over-plus land in the middle division (area of 1347 Tinkham Road).

In October 1744, Reverend Noah Merrick married his good friend's wife, widow Abigail (Fisk) Brainerd of Haddam, Connecticut. Abigail and Noah had seven children together. Abigail's six-year-old daughter, Abigail, from her previous marriage, was also part of the Merrick family, having eight children in total.

After much disagreement, a vote on the final location of the meeting house was held on March 15, 1748. Construction took place soon after, and the new meeting house was used later that year. The site was just southwest of Reverend Noah Merrick's home. From 1741 to the time the new meeting house was used, Nathaniel Hitchcock's home (603 Main Street) was used for precinct meetings and public worship.

On January 16, 1749, the inhabitants of Springfield Mountain chose three men—David Merrick, Isaac Brewer and Nathaniel Warriner—to be on a committee to represent the precinct to the Town of Springfield in taking action to set themselves off as a separate town. The Town of Springfield denied the request. Many other attempts were made, with the same results, until June 15, 1763, when the petition was finally granted. The Act of Incorporation was signed by Sir Francis Bernard, governor of the province.

Very few roads were laid out by the Town of Springfield within the precinct during these first twenty years. They were mere cart or bridle paths leading from one neighborhood or clearing to another. The only work that was done on these paths was to pick out some stones, make simple crossings over a few brooks and cut away the trees and brush that interfered with passing. The Bay Path was the only real road at the time in town, crossing west to east, which was created almost a century earlier.

It is said that after King Philip's War of 1675, many of the Native Americans in this area moved farther west, leaving this land to the European settlers. From local history, it is known that a few of the Native Americans stayed. One area known as Indian Rock was located just west of today's Hefferon Road in Wilbraham. It is said that a family or several Native Americans lived in this area and that some of them frequently came over into the center village, to Charles Brewer's tavern (473 Main Street), to procure supplies in the mid-1700s. Another, made famous in Wilbraham's history, was We-sha-u-gan, a Native American woman. Her wigwam, which gave the name to the hill where she lived, was on the east side of a small stream that divides the hill from the higher ground. This stream still flows today and can be seen in the clearing at the junction of Tinkham and Boles Roads.

We-sha-u-gan was an occasional visitor at Reverend Noah Merrick's home, which was located nearby. One time, Abigail, Noah's wife, and one of her children went to We-sha-u-gan's wigwam to eat succotash.

The following is a story that was written by Chauncey E. Peck in 1904. It's called "The Legend of Minneola." The meaning of *minneola* is "pleasant village." It's a story about Nathaniel Hitchcock and an interaction between him and We-sha-u-gan on Wigwam Hill. This is just one example of early life on Springfield Mountain:

> *On the afternoon of a day in mid-autumn, about the year 1745, Nathaniel Hitchcock, the first settler of Wilbraham, stood on Wigwam Hill. His trusty gun was by his side, and his well-filled bag of game showed that the day's hunt had been a success. He was on his way homeward. Down in the broad western valley at his feet, he had built his house of logs, fifteen years before. Neighbors now there were, but not then. He saw the smoke from the chimney of his log cabin, curling slowly upward on the still October day. It was a scene of peace. There his wife and children waiting for his coming for their evening meal, and there was plenty for their needs.*
>
> *Turning, he looked into the little valley southward. A moving form attracted his attention. It seemed to be a human figure, bent nearly double, darting quickly back and forth, apparently trying to catch something on the ground. He had seen it before. It was Weshaugan, the old Indian squaw, catching mice for her daily food. Weshaugan, the last of that mysterious race that had chased the deer over those hills; which had, in a crude way,*

Wilbraham Mountains, circa 1890. *Wilbraham Monson Academy.*

tilled those fields and had buried their dead within those valleys. Alone, deserted by her kindred, without tribesmen or tribe, she had lived there since the white men came.

He was stirred with pity for the lonely old woman and went down the hill toward her. She saw him coming and waited by her wigwam door. "Weshaugan," he said, "the day has yielded me more than plenty, and I am glad that it is so, for I can well spare you some of these birds." She took the two partridges he handed her, saying, "The white man is very kind, the white men have all been kind to We-sha-u-gan. More than once I have been invited, and have taken dinner at the minister's." With a slight show of pride she continued, "Only half a moon ago, I invited the minister and mistress to come to my table. I told them I had caught a nice, fat skunk for roasting, and wished them to taste the cooking of We-sha-u-gan. But the mistress explained that while I might eat at the minister's table, his position would not permit him to eat at mine. White folks have strange fancies."

She walked slowly back and forth before her wigwam for a moment, as though she did not wish the interview to end, and said, "White man, Weshaugan is growing old. The morning will soon dawn when she will not see its sunrise. The harvest moon is near, and at that time, for many generations, my people have told the legend of our tribe in this land, which we called Minnechoag, or Berry Land."

She motioned him to be seated on a shelf of rock that jutted out from a large boulder and seated herself upon a fallen tree trunk, her wigwam at her back, her body swaying slowly backward and forward the story proceeded, the lone old woman, the last one there of her people, told as THE LEGEND OF MINNEOLA.

A JOURNEY THROUGH CHILDHOOD MEMORIES AND THE TREASURES OF LOCAL HISTORY

The first twenty-three years of my life unfolded within the comforting embrace of 6 Chapel Street in North Wilbraham, a home that holds a treasure-trove of cherished memories. Situated in a neighborhood steeped in history, my upbringing was enriched by a deep love for local tales and traditions.

One particularly enchanting memory is the view from my bedroom window, a timeless snapshot of Sunday mornings when the church would come to life. The bells would create a symphony that resonated with the spirit of the community, fostering moments of quiet contemplation and instilling a profound appreciation for the cultural heartbeat echoing through the streets.

Equally mesmerizing were the stormy nights spent on the second-floor porch, where flashes of lightning vividly illuminated the historic Scotts property, once the Collins mill house and barn. These electrifying spectacles etched themselves into my memory, forming a web of experiences that connected me to the very essence of the place.

The neighborhood, adorned with nineteenth-century homes and barns, served as our playground. Each structure told a story of a bygone era, and as children, we explored the historic woods, tracing the footsteps of those who had traversed the long-forgotten roads of centuries past. It was a journey through time, where the whispers of history mingled with the laughter of our youth.

6 Chapel Street, circa 1890s. *Wilbraham Public Library.*

The old structures and historic woods weren't merely playgrounds—they were living chapters of a narrative that shaped my understanding of the world. As I reflect on those early years, I realize that my home wasn't just a physical space but rather a gateway to a rich memory and a profound love for the history that breathed life into it.

In the midst of this historical haven, two figures emerge as catalysts for my deeper exploration into the past: my next-door neighbors, Andy and Barbara Nygren. Their shared passion for history served as a beacon, illuminating my own journey into the layers of time that enveloped Wilbraham.

The Nygrens' residence at 3 Chapel Street stands as a living testament to bygone eras. Constructed in 1879 by Barbara's grandparents Erasmus B. and Harriet Gates, the house became an embodiment of the town's rich history. The Nygren home, more than a mere physical structure, evolved into a living museum curated by a family deeply connected to the town's past.

Andy and Barbara Nygren, avid historians themselves, generously shared the stories embedded within those walls, offering me a front-row seat to the fascinating history of Wilbraham. Their residence became a portal to the past, where each corner echoed with tales of a bygone era.

Through their guidance, I was able to witness and appreciate the intricate threads that wove together the fabric of Wilbraham's history. The Nygren home, with its living museum quality, served as a bridge between generations, connecting the present to the stories of the past. It was within those walls that I found inspiration and a deepened sense of connection to the historical roots that grounded me in the community. The Nygrens, with their unwavering dedication, became living embodiments of the vibrant history that unfolded within the charming town of Wilbraham.

Growing up in a profoundly historical part of town exposed me to myriad captivating features, from ancient roads and stone walls to remnants of trash dumps, each contributing to the richness of our community's past. It was within this historical landscape that my passion for collecting old bottles was kindled, thanks in large part to the guidance of Andy Nygren, a fellow enthusiast in the hobby.

Andy generously shared his knowledge and expertise with me, fostering a love for uncovering these tangible pieces of history. Together, we explored the hidden corners of our neighborhood, discovering treasures buried beneath layers of time. His mentorship not only deepened my appreciation for the hobby but also enriched my understanding of the historical significance embedded in each artifact.

As kids, our curiosity extended beyond bottles, leading us to explore the old houses and barns that dotted the neighborhood. Many of these structures retained the charm of yesteryear, preserving a tangible connection to the history that unfolded within their walls. The creaking floorboards and weathered beams whispered stories of generations long gone, making each exploration a journey through time.

We were indeed fortunate to have grown up in such a wonderful neighborhood, where history wasn't confined to textbooks but lived and breathed through the very landscapes we traversed. Our childhood adventures were not only filled with the thrill of discovery but also shaped by the genuine sense of wonder inspired by the historical richness surrounding us. The old houses and barns, the hidden relics in the earth and the shared enthusiasm of neighbors like Andy and Barbara Nygren collectively painted a vivid portrait of a community deeply rooted in its past—an upbringing that laid the foundation for a lifelong appreciation of history and the treasures it conceals.

The transformation of our neighborhood, although it still maintains its mid- to late nineteenth-century charm, is evident when one reflects on the changes that have unfolded from the early 1960s to the mid-1980s. However, it's crucial to remember that the historical roots of this area reach much further back, dating to the circa 1636 Old Bay Path.

In those early days, the landscape differed significantly from the perception of a dense forest with thick underbrush. Contrary to such assumptions, the land was open and passable in nearly every direction. Native Americans played a crucial role in shaping this environment by practicing controlled burns each year, promoting the growth of grass and berry bushes to attract deer. The only areas of dense forest were in swampy regions untouched by these fires. This intentional management created a landscape where people and wildlife could move freely.

The Old Bay Path, often associated with William Pynchon's original journey from the Bay Colony to Springfield circa 1636, was originally thought to follow a "Great Indian trail." However, historical accuracy reveals that Pynchon arrived by ship, circumventing the cape and sailing up the Connecticut River to Springfield. The subsequent creation of the

Bay Path was driven by travelers heading east to the Bay Colony, marking the beginning of a significant highway. The Connecticut Path served as the primary route to the expansive river in the west, connecting the Bay Colony to the Connecticut settlements of Wethersfield, Windsor and Hartford. Naturally, both of these pathways originated as Native American trails.

In these early times, Native Americans navigated the landscape at will, using footpaths established by long use to connect settlements and seasonal camps. These paths, not always the most direct routes, were designed for ease and convenience, avoiding steep hills and crossing streams at shallow fords. They led to spring sites for gathering plants and fishing, as well as to summer corn fields.

Reflecting on this history offers a profound perspective on the evolution of our neighborhood, reminding us that the pathways we tread today carry the echoes of centuries-old footprints and the thoughtful interactions between the land and its stewards. Even General George Washington himself and many other notable people passed through this very locale.

Chapel Street, aptly named after the construction of the church in 1877, has a historical foundation dating back to the eighteenth century. By 1839, two houses adorned the lower section toward Boston Road, although both have long since disappeared. Early maps indicate the presence of two barns, one on each side of the street, likely associated with these former residences.

The dynamics of Chapel Street underwent significant changes around the mid-nineteenth century. The burgeoning population in this part of town, particularly from the 1870s onward, can be attributed to various factors, including the building of the Western Railroad in 1839 with relocation of the railroad station in 1851, the establishment of Collins Paper Company in 1872, the Cutler Company in 1876 and the construction of Grace Chapel Parish of Collins Depot in 1877. This influx of businesses and institutions brought about an increased demand for workers at all levels, prompting a migration of individuals to the area.

With the industrial and civic developments, Chapel Street, along with other areas of this neighborhood, became a hub for both residence and commerce. The growth of the community was accompanied by the establishment of various businesses, including a cheese factory, several stores, a hotel, a blacksmith shop and a livery stable. These enterprises not only catered to the needs of the burgeoning population but also contributed to the vibrant economic and social life of this area.

The historical evolution encapsulates the transformations driven by industrial and community developments, shaping the landscape and character of the neighborhood. Today, this area stands as a testament to its rich heritage, with each step echoing the footsteps of those who contributed to its growth and prosperity over the centuries.

Charles and Helen Stacy, dynamic pioneers of their time, made a lasting mark on Chapel Street by constructing their residence at 6 Chapel Street in 1878, the home where I grew up. Remarkably, they undertook this endeavor at the youthful ages of twenty-nine and thirty. It's noteworthy that while Charles was not directly associated with the burgeoning mills in the area, his occupation as a beef dealer spoke to the diverse economic activities shaping the community.

Choosing a location adjacent to the newly constructed church, the Stacys became integral members of the community. Their house, standing proudly next to the church, bore witness to the evolving landscape of Chapel Street during this period of growth and transformation.

Charles Stacy's contributions extended beyond his role as a beef dealer and homeowner. Actively engaged in local government, he assumed the position of Wilbraham town clerk, serving from 1880 to 1885 and again from 1891 to 1897. His dedication to public service showcased a commitment to the well-being and progress of the town.

Charles Garvin, the subsequent owner of the house at 6 Chapel Street, brought with him a background rooted in the paper industry. Having relocated from Agawam to Wilbraham, Charles found employment in the Collins paper mills, continuing a family tradition. In Agawam, he worked alongside his father, Orrin, who held the position of a paper mill supervisor.

Charles's tenure in the Chapel Street residence, along with his mother, Sarah, was relatively brief. They lived there for only a few years until 1901. Subsequently, Charles and Sarah made another move, this time to Newburgh, New York. Garvin's journey reflects the transient nature of life during that era, with individuals often relocating to pursue opportunities or adapt to changing circumstances.

The house at 6 Chapel Street became a temporary haven for Charles Garvin and his mother, witnessing a chapter in their lives influenced by industrial work, familial connections and the ever-changing landscape of early twentieth-century America. As they moved on to new horizons, the house retained the echoes of their presence, contributing to the historical layers that continue to shape Chapel Street.

The next chapter in the history of 6 Chapel Street saw the arrival of Dr. Arthur L. and Grace Damon, notable figures in Wilbraham's community. Dr. Damon, one of the town's most respected and beloved general practitioners, dedicated nearly five decades of service to the people during the first half of the twentieth century. Not only did the house become their home, but it also served as Dr. Damon's office.

Beyond his medical practice, Dr. Damon actively engaged in civic responsibilities. He demonstrated his commitment to the town by serving as a dedicated library trustee from 1910 to 1942. His enduring contributions to the community through both his medical expertise and civic involvement solidified his status as a revered figure in Wilbraham.

While Dr. and Mrs. Damon did not have children of their own, family ties remained an important aspect of their lives. In the 1940s, Dr. Damon's sister-in-law became part of their household, creating a familial atmosphere within the walls of 6 Chapel Street.

The Damon residence stands as a testament to the intersection of professional dedication, community service and family bonds. Dr. Arthur L. Damon's legacy lived on in the memories of those he served and the town he enriched through his medical practice and civic contributions. The house, with its years of medical practice and family life, became a cornerstone in Wilbraham's rich history.

Dr. Damon's residency marked a transformative period, as he undertook several alterations to the house in 1901, giving it a distinctly eclectic character. Originally an Italianate-style two-story house with a pyramidal, hipped roof, the residence took on new features under Dr. Damon's influence.

One significant addition was the incorporation of a corner tower, a distinctive architectural element that altered the house's original Italianate design. This tower served a dual purpose, enhancing the overall aesthetic of the structure while providing space for Dr. Damon's medical office on the first floor and two bedrooms on the second floor.

Around 1920, further modifications were made to the southwest corner of the house. An English cottage–style, fully enclosed portico with a sloping roof was added, contributing to the evolving nature of the architecture. With this addition, an exterior chimney to the north side was added, adding both functionality and visual interest to the structure.

The exterior shingle siding, likely added around the same time as the portico, further contributed to the eclectic appearance of the house. This period of architectural evolution reflects the changing tastes and needs of the Damon family, blending different styles seamlessly and creating a unique and personalized aesthetic.

The home at 6 Chapel Street—with its Italianate roots, corner tower, English cottage-style portico and exterior shingle siding—stands as a testament to the dynamic nature of architectural evolution and the personal touches that shape a home over time. Each addition and alteration carry a piece of the Damon family's history and the evolving character of Wilbraham's architectural landscape.

The architectural features of 6 Chapel Street reveal a fascinating history of alterations and additions, mirroring the changes in the tastes and needs of its occupants over the years. Similar to its neighbor at 4 Chapel Street, this house includes a rear ell, a common architectural element during its original construction in 1878. However, notable modifications have occurred, contributing to its distinctive character.

The rear ell initially had a pitched roof, a characteristic of its 1878 construction. Subsequent alterations, likely associated with the addition of the corner tower, resulted in changes to the roof, which was raised to accommodate the evolving architectural elements.

Around 1920, further enhancements took place, adding to the charm of the house. A glassed-in corner porch on the second floor, located on the north side, and the enclosure of the first-floor porch below were introduced during this period. These additions not only expanded the living space but also added unique and personalized features to the overall design.

In keeping with its neighbor at 4 Chapel Street, 6 Chapel Street has retained its two-story barn and attached one-story carriage shed. These ancillary structures, often integral to properties of this era, provide a glimpse into the historical functionality and lifestyle of the home.

The historical timeline of 6 Chapel Street continues with Roger and Gail Whitehill, who lived in one of the three apartments within the home back in 1955. During this period, Grace Damon still owned the property, and the Whitehills experienced a chapter in the house's multifaceted history.

In 1959, a pivotal moment in the property's ownership occurred when Grace Damon sold the house to Robert Dietz for approximately $18,500. This transaction was considered a substantial sum of money for that time. The house—having already witnessed numerous alterations, occupants and historical events—continued to adapt to the shifting dynamics of Wilbraham. The Whitehills' residency and Grace Damon's decision to sell the property to Robert Dietz further enrich the stories of this historical home.

The addition of Robert Dietz to the ownership of 6 Chapel Street brings another layer of history, intertwining the property with the town's firefighting legacy. As a member of the Wilbraham Fire Department, Robert Dietz was already deeply connected to the community's safety and well-being. While owning 6 Chapel Street, Robert continued to maintain his home in the center of town. His dedication to the fire department and the community eventually culminated in him ascending to the role of fire chief for Wilbraham.

The story of 6 Chapel Street intertwines with my own journey in a profound way, as I was born in one of its apartments in 1962. My family's connection to this historic home became an integral part of our lives. The owner, Robert Dietz, not only provided a place to live but also recruited my father into the Wilbraham Fire Department, where he would eventually retire as a call fire lieutenant in 1993.

So this house, nestled in the heart of a vibrant and historic neighborhood, played a pivotal role in shaping the person I am today. The early exposure to the fire service ignited a passion that has endured throughout my life. Over the span of thirty-seven and a half years, I proudly served as a member of the Wilbraham Fire Department, eventually retiring as fire chief in 2019.

The love for history, cultivated in the very fabric of this community, has seamlessly transitioned into a guiding force during my retirement years. This enduring connection to both the fire service and the rich history of the neighborhood and town continues to shape and enrich my life today.

The supernatural experiences recounted from 6 Chapel Street are undeniably intriguing. Over the years, these tales have captivated the imagination of many, leaving an indelible mark on those who have encountered the inexplicable.

The narrative begins with my mother's encounter many years ago with a spectral figure cloaked in blue, seemingly suspended above the ground between the church and our house. The image of this ethereal lady, clutching her mysterious purse, haunts the memory, etched into our family's history.

In more recent times, the house has continued to be a nexus of peculiar occurrences. Witnesses have described a woman in a white nightgown, her form seemingly weightless as she drifts atop the front staircase—a manifestation both eerie and mesmerizing. Even the resident cats, with their keen senses, have been drawn to the enigmatic presence, their gaze following unseen movements in the same vicinity.

The palpable sensation of a feminine presence, accompanied by a gentle coolness that somehow exudes warmth, has enveloped certain occupants, offering a curious blend of comfort and intrigue. And while some have experienced the inexplicable sensation of their bed covers being gently pulled off, there's an underlying feeling of benign intent, as if the ethereal visitor seeks only acknowledgment.

Across the street, the mystery deepens with sightings of a child in the window of the turret of the old Cutler house, a fleeting apparition that vanishes as quickly as it appears. These sightings, shrouded in uncertainty, add another layer to the supernatural lore throughout our town.

Indeed, the tales that swirl around 6 Chapel Street and its environs serve as a testament to the enduring fascination with the unknown. With each retelling, the mysteries deepen, leaving us to ponder the existence of realms beyond our understanding and the enduring presence of spirits that tread the line between our world and the next.

NEWBURY DITCHES OF 1729

The area that is now the town of Wilbraham and Hampden has a rich history dating back to the settlement of Agawam Plantation. In 1636, William Pynchon and his associates acquired the land, then known as "Agawam." The name was officially changed to Springfield in 1640, named after Pynchon's home village in Essex, England.

The original lands of the town of Springfield covered approximately twenty-five square miles. This territory extended from the Connecticut River to the east as far as the present line of Monson and Palmer, west to the area of Russell and from the southern town line of Enfield and Warehouse Point, Connecticut, to the mountains of Holyoke to the north.

The eastern lands, lying beyond the established settlement along the eastern shore of the Connecticut River, were referred to as the Inner and Outward Commons. These lands were part of Pynchon's original purchase and had not been specifically allocated to any of the inhabitants of Springfield. These common lands were open for use by all, including Native Americans, for activities such as hunting, fishing, foraging and obtaining resources like grass, herbage and timber.

Around 1684, there was a growing concern among the settlers that Sir Edmund Andros, the governor of Massachusetts, might revoke the colony's charter. Andros had threatened to take away the charter, which could result in all unappropriated lands reverting back to the authority of King Charles II of England. This situation added a layer of uncertainty and anxiety among the residents of Springfield, as they faced the potential loss of their communal lands and the freedoms associated with them.

On February 3, 1685, a significant town meeting took place where a crucial decision was made regarding the division of land in Springfield. The meeting concluded with a vote to distribute the land among the 122 heads of families. However, before this division, certain portions of land were reserved for specific purposes, including acreage for their revered teacher, Pelatiah Glover, as well as for ministry and school lots. In total, 125 land grants were established for each of the three divisions.

Importantly, these land grants were allocated without any form of compensation, and the only condition attached was that the recipient should remain a citizen and make use of the land. Failure to comply with this condition could result in forfeiture of the granted land. The grants were a means of encouraging settlement and community development.

It's worth noting that the survey conducted in 1726 played a crucial role in definitively fixing the portions allocated to the proprietors in 1685. This survey helped establish clear boundaries and ownership, providing a formalized structure for the distribution of land.

Remarkably, despite the land being divided in 1685, it took forty-six years for the first settlers to occupy the area on a full-time basis. This delay could be attributed to various factors, such as the gradual growth and development of the community, economic considerations or external challenges faced by the settlers. Nonetheless, this delayed occupation marks a significant period in the history of the region.

The historical map drawn up by Henry Edson in 1917 provides valuable insights into the layout and distribution of the divided numbered lots in the second and third divisions of the Outward Commons of Springfield. This map serves as a visual representation of the land grants made in 1685, offering a glimpse into the historical geography of the area.

Additionally, Peck's 1913 history is a valuable resource that complements the map by providing the names of individuals who were granted these lots. This historical record not only adds a personal dimension to the land distribution but also helps trace the lineage and settlement patterns of the early inhabitants.

Beyond the allocation of lots, the map includes other relevant information and points of interest, contributing to a comprehensive understanding of the historical landscape. This includes landmarks, community structures, events or geographical features that held significance in the development of the town.

Combining the map with Peck's historical account provides a multidimensional view of the community's past, allowing researchers, historians and residents to connect with the specific individuals and families who played a role in shaping the region.

To recap, the Outward Commons were divided into three divisions on the east side of the Connecticut River and two divisions on the west side, totaling five divisions. Each division measured about four miles square, resulting in an overall area about twelve miles long from north to south and four miles wide from east to west.

The first division, located in the north, covered a substantial portion of what is now Ludlow. The second or middle division extended from Ludlow, just north of the Chicopee River, to the southern part of Wilbraham, stopping just south of Tinkham Road. The third division continued south from this line, encompassing what is now Hampden, extending to the Massachusetts and Connecticut border. It's worth noting that there was some confusion about the proximity of the Connecticut line in the Outward Commons during that period.

The width from east to west spanned from the town line of Brimfield (now Monson and Palmer) to approximately where Stony Hill Road is today. Parts of Stony Hill Road crossed into the Inner Commons, which extended from the Outward Commons, westward, to the settled portions of Springfield, often referred to as the "Plains."

Each one of the grantees would be allowed one track of land, a lot, in each of the five divisions. These lots are numbered, beginning at the north side of each division; the north lot is 1, the next 2 and so on up to 125. At the south end of each division will be land called the over-plus land. This land was extra in case it was needed due to survey errors.

Each lot granted in all five divisions would be in accordance with estates and polls. In the three divisions on the east side of the river, all lots were to be four miles long, east to west, and the width would be determined by one's wealth. There was much disparity in width sizes; for example, Colonel Pynchon's lot 2 in the second division was 2,143 feet and 9 inches wide, while William Brooks's lot 111 in the second division was 8 feet and 9 inches wide—both lots being four miles long. It was said that a wagon could not turn around on these small lots without trespassing on another property. One could imagine how it would be difficult to build a home and farm the land on a lot of this size. But you would have to remember that this was all done to save the land from reverting back to the king. Most of these lots were purchased many years later by other settlers who purchased multiple lots to gain more width. It would take another forty-five years until the first settler, Nathaniel Hitchcock, established his part-time homestead here in the Outward Commons in 1730. In May 1731, he would permanently reside here with his wife, whom he married that year. Nathaniel Hitchcock purchased lot 123, located in the second division, which was originally granted to Nathaniel Burt. This lot was 368 feet, 4 inches in width and four miles long. He built his home at what is now 603 Main Street, Wilbraham.

In the spring of 1717, the settlers of Springfield took a significant step toward establishing clear boundaries within their cherished Inner and Outward Commons. On April 1 of that year, a committee—composed of notable figures including Colonel John Pynchon, Lieutenant William Pynchon, Mr. Glover and Mr. Parsons—was appointed with the crucial task of defining the line between the Inner and Outward Commons.

Despite the importance of this endeavor, historical records unfortunately reveal no evidence of a survey being conducted until the arrival of Lieutenant Roger Newbury in 1729. Lieutenant Newbury, recognized for his expertise as a surveyor, was engaged by the Committee for the Proprietors of the Springfield Eastern Outward Commons to undertake this vital task.

The committee, under Newbury's guidance, entrusted him with the responsibility of determining the north–south length of the Outward Commons and subsequently dividing them into three equal portions. Additionally, his mandate included establishing a definitive line between the Inner and Outward Commons, a crucial demarcation to bring clarity to the land divisions.

This sign commemorates Newbury's boundary line of 1729. Location of this sign is between 501 and 511 Springfield Street. *David F. Bourcier.*

From May 20 to May 22, 1729, Lieutenant Roger Newbury diligently executed the survey, leaving a lasting imprint on the landscape. To mark the boundaries of each division and the line between the Inner and Outward Commons, Newbury employed stone heaps and dug ditches. Over time, these distinctive ditches, etched into the land with precision, became known as the Newbury Ditches.

Today, remnants of Lieutenant Roger Newbury's meticulous survey endure, as these historic ditches and stone heaps persist on the untouched lands of Wilbraham and Hampden. They serve not only as tangible markers of the early settlers' efforts to define and protect their commons but also as a testament to the enduring legacy of those who shaped the landscape for generations to come.

MARY BLISS PARSONS, ACCUSED OF WITCHCRAFT

In the tumultuous landscape of seventeenth-century New England, a pervasive belief in the existence of witches gripped the minds of virtually every inhabitant. The era bore witness to a grim chapter in history where hundreds of individuals found themselves ensnared in the web of accusations surrounding the practice of witchcraft. The accused were predominantly women, and occasionally men, who were alleged to have "signed the Devil's Book" and were purportedly carrying out nefarious deeds in the service of the dark forces.

This widespread hysteria attributed myriad calamities, from ailing livestock to the tragic demise of infant children, to the perceived malevolence of these accused witches. Despite the fact that many faced charges, the majority never stood trial, and some, like Mary Parsons, managed to secure acquittal. However, fortune did not smile on everyone during this dark period. Six women in Massachusetts met a grim fate at the hands of the justice system, being hanged as witches in the years preceding the infamous Salem witch trials—a harrowing event that ultimately claimed the lives of twenty-four innocent individuals. The echoes of this troubled era resonate through history, serving as a stark reminder of the profound impact of superstition and fear on the course of human lives.

In the year 1646, the union of Mary Bliss and Joseph Parsons marked the commencement of a life journey intertwined with the evolving landscape of colonial America. Their nuptials, solemnized in Hartford, set the stage for a familial odyssey that would traverse the burgeoning settlements of

Springfield and, eventually, the nascent community of Northampton, situated some twenty miles up the meandering Connecticut River.

Mary Bliss Parsons was the great-aunt of Abel Bliss, a noteworthy figure among the early settlers of the Outward Commons, now recognized as Wilbraham. In the year 1736, Abel, alongside his wife, Jemima Chapin, forged a new beginning in this scenic locale, establishing roots and nurturing a family of five children.

As the Parsons family expanded to include three children, they embarked on a new chapter in Northampton, where Joseph Parsons swiftly ascended the ranks to become a prominent figure in the community. Beyond the confines of familial responsibilities, he emerged as a triumphant merchant, leveraging his success to contribute actively to the development of Northampton. Joseph's civic engagement manifested through roles as a selectman and a vital participant in the committee entrusted with the construction of the town's inaugural meeting house. The Parsons homestead became a pivotal hub in the vibrant settlement of Northampton, not only due to Joseph's civic involvement but also owing to the family's ownership of the town's inaugural tavern.

In a parallel trajectory to the Parsons, the lives of Sarah and James Bridgman unfolded along a similar path, commencing with their union in Hartford. The couple embarked on a journey that mirrored the northward expansion of colonial settlements, first finding themselves in Springfield before venturing farther to Northampton. However, unlike the harmonious course of the Parsons' familial narrative, the Bridgmans encountered a starkly different and tumultuous experience.

As the Bridgmans set down roots in Northampton, an unforeseen turn of events unfolded when a feud materialized between their family and the Parsons. Mary Parsons and Sarah Bridgman found themselves entwined in a fateful tale against the backdrop of suspicion and whispers. Shortly after Mary gave birth to a son, an event celebrated as the arrival of the first English child in the burgeoning town, a shadow was cast over the joyous occasion.

Tragedy struck when Sarah Bridgman also welcomed a newborn into the world. However, the infant's untimely demise within a mere two weeks cast a pall over the community. In the wake of this sorrow, Sarah, grappling with grief, made a startling claim that Mary Parsons's alleged witchcraft was the sinister force behind her child's premature passing.

The winds of rumor began to swirl through the tightknit town of Northampton, carrying whispers of supernatural involvement and dark accusations. Unwilling to let these insinuations go unchallenged, Joseph

Parsons, Mary's husband, took a bold stance. In a move fraught with risk, he decided to go on the offensive, charging James Bridgman with slander for perpetuating rumors about Mary's purported witchcraft.

In an era when juries typically sided with the plaintiff in such cases, Joseph Parsons ventured into treacherous territory by bringing the incendiary rumors to the attention of the authorities. The gamble lay in the possibility that officials might give credence to the accusations, potentially turning the plaintiff into an unexpected defendant. The tense atmosphere in Northampton underscored the delicate balance between superstition and justice.

The gripping saga of Mary Parsons's alleged witchcraft and the ensuing legal battle reached its climax at the Magistrates' Court in Cambridge in October 1656. The courtroom buzzed with anticipation as thirty-three depositions were presented, offering a mosaic of perspectives on the mysterious and haunting events that had unfolded in the town of Northampton.

A remarkable turnout from the community marked the proceedings, with almost half of Northampton's thirty-two households dispatching witnesses to testify. Some came even from neighboring Springfield, reflecting the gravity and widespread impact of the accusations. The court became a stage where personal grievances, suspicions and the supernatural collided, weaving a complex narrative that would be scrutinized by the magistrates.

Central to the case was Sarah Bridgman, who recounted a chilling tale that unfolded in May 1654. She spoke of a resounding "great blow on the door" that reverberated through the air of her home, a prelude to an ominous shift in the well-being of her newborn child. A disturbing vision unfolded as she claimed to witness "two women pass by the door with white clothes on their heads," only for them to vanish into the ether. Sarah, gripped by a sense of foreboding, concluded that her son's fate was sealed, convinced that the presence of malevolent forces and "wickedness in the place" would bring about his demise.

As the courtroom absorbed these accounts, the intricate web of supernatural beliefs, fear and personal vendettas played out in a legal arena where the line between superstition and evidence blurred. The depositions illuminated the challenges of adjudicating such cases, where the ethereal and the tangible collided in a quest for justice and resolution. The trial became a microcosm of the era's complexities, shedding light on the intersection of the supernatural and the judicial system in seventeenth-century New England.

Witness after witness presented accounts following a familiar script—an argument or disagreement would occur, and when misfortune befell them later, the blame was swiftly attributed to witchcraft. Such causal connections, often fueled by fear and suspicion, were considered valid evidence in the eyes of the court.

One woman, for instance, detailed how the yarn she had spun for Mary Parsons inexplicably ended up full of knots. Drawing a peculiar conclusion based on this occurrence, she asserted that the knots were a direct result of Mary's alleged witchcraft, as the yarn she spun for others remained pristine and knot-free.

Similarly, another woman linked her daughter's sudden illness to a refusal to let the girl work for Mary Parsons. The sequence of events, from the denial of labor to the onset of illness, became a thread in the narrative connecting Mary Parsons to the perceived malevolence that plagued the community.

A male witness contributed his own account, stating that after an exchange of discontented words with Mary Parsons, he discovered his cow in the yard on the verge of death the following day. The cow's demise, occurring two weeks later, was, in his eyes, a consequence of the discord between them.

Amid the swirl of accusations and spectral testimonies, a chorus of voices rose in Mary Parsons's defense during the trial. Three women stepped forward, offering a counter-narrative to Sarah Bridgman's account. They attested that Sarah's baby had been unwell from the moment of birth, challenging the notion that Mary's alleged witchcraft was the cause of the child's affliction.

Further support for Parsons emerged from a neighbor who provided a different perspective on the fate of the disputed cow. Contrary to the notion of supernatural influence, the neighbor asserted that the cow had succumbed to a more mundane ailment—specifically, "water in the belly."

With these testimonies, a narrative of doubt and alternative explanations was woven into the fabric of the trial. The court, charged with untangling the threads of truth from the intricate web of beliefs and accusations, ultimately ruled in favor of Parsons. The Bridgmans, faced with the decision of either paying a fine or issuing a public apology, opted for the former, concluding the legal saga.

The long-standing feud and the harrowing ordeal of Mary Parsons experienced a resurgence eighteen years later, casting a shadow over her life once again in 1674. This time, the son-in-law of the Bridgmans filed a new complaint, expressing strong suspicions that his wife had met an untimely demise through unusual and possibly nefarious means—specifically, he suspected Mary Bliss Parsons to be involved.

On January 5, 1675, county magistrates summoned Mary Parsons to appear before them. The proceedings took a dark turn as women subjected her to a distressing examination, searching her body for the mythical "witch's teats"—unexplained protrusions where, according to seventeenth century beliefs, supernatural entities known as "imps" were said to suck. The historical record remains silent on the findings of this examination.

Despite the lack of surviving records from this trial, it is known that in March of the same year, the Court of Assistants in Boston decided to send Mary Parsons to prison to await trial. The trial itself is shrouded in historical mystery, with no surviving documents to recount the proceedings. However, a pivotal moment arrived on May 13, 1675, when a jury declared Mary Parsons not guilty.

Despite the acquittal, the specter of suspicion lingered. In 1679 or 1680, the Parsons family chose to relocate from Northampton back to Springfield, perhaps seeking respite from the persistent rumors that continued to haunt them. Mary Bliss Parsons, resilient in the face of adversity, lived well into her mid-eighties and passed away in 1712. Her life—marked by accusations, trials and relocations—stands as a testament to the enduring challenges faced by individuals entangled in the web of witchcraft accusations during this period in colonial New England.

Mary Parsons's experience, though distinguished by her relatively secure social position as the wife of one of the wealthiest and most respected men

ILLUSTRATION BY BLANCHE CYBELE DERBY, 1995

Illustration of Mary Bliss Parsons by Blanche Cybele Derby.

in Western Massachusetts, aligned with the prevailing norms of the time. Her case exemplified a recurring pattern in the accusations of witchcraft that unfolded in early New England.

It's noteworthy that middle-aged women, including Mary Parsons, were disproportionately targeted by accusations of witchcraft during this period. Despite her social standing, she found herself ensnared in the complex web of suspicions and superstitions that plagued many women of her demographic.

Moreover, the issues of jealousy, personal animosity and familial disputes that played a prominent role in Mary Parsons's ordeal foreshadowed the dark turn that the Salem witch hysteria of 1692 would take. The same potent combination of interpersonal conflicts, societal tensions and deep-seated fears would fuel the mass hysteria that gripped Salem, resulting in numerous accusations, trials and tragic executions.

Mary Parsons's story serves as a microcosm of the broader societal dynamics at play during an era when accusations of witchcraft could disrupt the lives of even those in privileged positions. Her experience resonates as a cautionary tale, highlighting the vulnerability of individuals, particularly women, to the capricious and often unfounded suspicions that characterized a tumultuous chapter in colonial New England history.

LETTERS THROUGH WILBRAHAM

TRACING THE PIONEERING POSTAL ROUTE

The Boston Post Road, also known as the Upper Post Road, stands as the pioneering postal route linking Boston and New York City, traversing through Wilbraham. It represents a significant historical artery alongside two other notable routes: the Lower Post Road and the Middle Post Road. Over time, segments of these pivotal postal roads evolved into prominent trails and pathways, laying the groundwork for several U.S. and interstate routes.

The Upper Post Road, the oldest among the designated trio, boasted the highest traffic volume. Its path roughly aligns with present-day U.S. Route 5 and U.S. Route 20. Conversely, the Lower Post Road hugs the coastline from New York to Connecticut before veering north through Providence, Rhode Island, en route to Boston. Portions of the Lower Post Road roughly correspond to the original alignment of U.S. Route 1 across eastern Connecticut, Rhode Island and Massachusetts. Meanwhile, the Middle Post Road, the most direct and expedient route from New York to Boston, emerges as the oldest pathway but youngest segment of the designated postal routes. Its trajectory loosely mirrors that of today's U.S. Route 44 and U.S. Route 16. Interestingly, this route marked the inaugural trail, the Connecticut Path, where pioneering settlers from Boston ventured inland, drawn by the allure of the majestic Connecticut River Valley. It was along this path that they forged their way to establish the first vibrant settlements now recognized as Hartford, Windsor and Wethersfield, Connecticut.

Preceding the arrival of European settlers in North America, Native Americans forged trails that saw frequent use, eventually integrating into segments of post roads essential for mail delivery to early colonists. The inception of the Boston Post Road dates back to 1673, when the first sections were laid out, marking America's inaugural mail route. Throughout the 1700s, intrepid riders traversed the Boston Post Road, carrying the *Boston News Letter*, heralded as America's inaugural regular newspaper, alongside routine mail deliveries. This facilitated the dissemination of information among settlers and fostered the interconnection of towns dotting the route.

In 1753, Elliot Benger, the postmaster general for the colonies, retired from his position, paving the way for Benjamin Franklin and William Hunter to assume the mantle of responsibility. While ostensibly sharing the role of postmaster general, in reality, Benjamin Franklin emerged as the driving force behind the management of the colonial postal system, which operated under the auspices of the British government. Franklin's ambitious vision and proactive approach propelled him into a leadership position, guiding the direction and operations of the postal service during this pivotal period in colonial history.

It was written that, facing his initial challenge, Benjamin Franklin embarked on a crucial journey in the summer of 1753, a decade before Wilbraham's incorporation as a town. His mission was to dispel the suspicions of his Yankee customers, who harbored doubts about the fairness of postage fees assessed by the mile. To tackle this issue head-on, Franklin embarked on a remarkable five-month expedition, meticulously surveying the postal roads utilized for mail delivery, including the original Upper Post Road, which traversed the area now known as Wilbraham.

To ensure the most efficient routes for mail delivery, Franklin ingeniously devised an odometer, a groundbreaking invention for its time. This device, attached to his wagon, precisely measured the distance traveled by counting the revolutions of the wheels. Throughout his journey, spanning approximately 1,600 miles of postal roads, Franklin's odometer meticulously recorded the distance covered along each route. To mark each mile, stakes were driven into the ground, while a dedicated crew followed behind, erecting durable stone markers along the surveyed paths.

Franklin's exhaustive efforts not only provided concrete evidence of the actual distances traveled along postal routes but also helped instill confidence among customers regarding the fairness of postage assessments. His innovative approach to surveying and his commitment to transparency laid a solid foundation for the efficient operation of the colonial postal system, ensuring reliable mail delivery and fostering trust among the communities it served.

In recent years, there has been controversy surrounding the claim that Benjamin Franklin personally laid out or ordered the placement of roadside milestones. Some argue that U.S. Post Office officials, including Franklin, had neither the responsibility nor the budget to build and maintain roads, bridges, ferries or milestones. As a result, the exact truth of Franklin's involvement remains uncertain, and we may never fully uncover the facts.

On October 20, 1783, a pivotal moment in transportation history unfolded as the Boston Post Road, also referred to as the Upper Post Road, facilitated America's inaugural long-distance stagecoach and mail service connecting New York and Boston. This milestone marked a significant leap forward in the efficiency and accessibility of transportation across the young nation.

At the forefront of this transformative endeavor stood Levi Pease, a remarkable figure hailing from Connecticut. A skilled blacksmith and distinguished war veteran, Pease played a crucial role in various specialized functions during the Revolutionary War. His responsibilities encompassed transportation-related tasks, including the delivery of correspondence, procurement of horses and procurement of provisions for the army. Pease's unwavering dedication and resourcefulness significantly contributed to the logistical success of the military operations during this tumultuous period.

However, Pease's contributions did not end with the cessation of hostilities. In the subsequent years, he leveraged his expertise and experience to revolutionize mail delivery services throughout the United States. Pease's visionary initiatives and innovative spirit laid the groundwork for advancements in the transportation industry that resonated well into the twentieth century.

Following the Revolutionary War, Levi Pease capitalized on his intimate knowledge of transportation routes and the New England region by embarking on a new venture. In 1783, he launched his first transportation route, linking Somers and Hartford, Connecticut, leveraging his expertise to establish a reliable connection between these two pivotal locations.

Recognizing the potential for expansion and eager to further enhance transportation and mail delivery services, Pease set his sights on a grander ambition: establishing a route spanning from Boston to New York City. However, such an endeavor necessitated both financial backing and a capable business partner.

In his search for a suitable collaborator, Pease turned to his trusted friend Reuben Sykes, whose credentials as a blacksmith and tavern owner made him an ideal candidate for the partnership. Sykes, born in Springfield,

Massachusetts, operated a tavern situated along the Boston Post Road, located at what is now 40 Maple Street in Wilbraham.

The collaboration between Pease and Sykes marked the inception of a pioneering enterprise, with each man undertaking the arduous journey from their respective starting points—Hartford and Boston—at approximately the same time. This synchronized approach ensured the efficient and timely delivery of both passengers and mail between the two bustling cities.

Together, Pease and Sykes forged a pathway for improved connectivity and commerce along the bustling thoroughfare of the Boston Post Road, laying the groundwork for the expansion of transportation networks and the facilitation of vital communication across state lines. Their partnership exemplified the spirit of entrepreneurship and collaboration that characterized the early pioneers of America's burgeoning transportation industry.

The introduction of the stagecoach service along the Boston Post Road marked a turning point in long-distance travel, providing passengers with a more comfortable and expedient means of transportation between two major cities. The success of this stagecoach service not only revolutionized travel along the route but also underscored the importance of further infrastructure enhancements to support burgeoning transportation needs.

Moreover, the reliability and efficiency demonstrated by the stagecoach and mail service on the Boston Post Road garnered the attention of Congress. Recognizing the potential benefits of utilizing stagecoaches for mail delivery, Congress made the momentous decision to transition from solitary riders to stagecoach transport for mail services. This shift not only expedited mail delivery but also contributed to the overall development of a more organized and dependable postal system across the nation.

Thus, the convergence of advancements in road infrastructure and the introduction of stagecoach services along the Boston Post Road paved the way for significant improvements in long-distance transportation and mail delivery, laying the groundwork for further innovations in America's evolving transportation network.

In the autumn of 1789, following his inauguration as the first president of the United States, George Washington embarked on a historic tour along the famed Boston Post Road from New York to Boston. This journey through New England carried profound significance, symbolizing the new nation's unity and the president's commitment to forging strong ties with its diverse regions.

President Washington's tour commenced with his arrival in Springfield, Massachusetts, where he commenced his exploration of New England.

His first official stop in Massachusetts was Springfield, where he inspected the federal arsenal, underscoring the importance of national defense and security.

Continuing his journey, President Washington's entourage traversed through Wilbraham and other various towns and villages along the Boston Post Road, including notable stops in Palmer, West Brookfield, Brookfield, Spencer, Leicester and Worcester. At each juncture, he was met with enthusiastic receptions and expressions of respect from the local populace.

One particularly memorable moment occurred upon his arrival in Worcester, where President Washington was greeted with a resounding thirteen-gun salute, a gesture of honor and reverence befitting his esteemed position.

Pressing onward, President Washington's itinerary carried him through Marlborough, Shrewsbury, Sudbury and Weston before reaching his destination of Cambridge. Notably, Cambridge held special significance for President Washington, having served as his headquarters during the pivotal Siege of Boston in the early stages of the Revolutionary War.

Upon his arrival in Cambridge, President Washington was greeted with great pomp and ceremony, as Lieutenant Governor Samuel Adams and the Executive Council welcomed him with utmost respect and honor. President Washington's diary reflects his appreciation for the warm reception, describing the occasion as "flattering & honorable" in every regard.

President Washington's journey along the Boston Post Road underscored his commitment to unity, reconciliation and the cultivation of strong bonds between the federal government and the diverse regions of the fledgling nation. His historic tour left an indelible mark on the collective memory of the American people, symbolizing the promise of a united and prosperous future under the leadership of the nation's first president.

Benjamin Franklin as postmaster general. *Philadelphia History Museum at the Atwater Kent/Bridgeman Images.*

A charming anecdote from a letter penned by Antonette Catherine Mary Bliss (Speer) on December 30, 1878, reveals a delightful connection between her family and one of America's most iconic figures. According to Antonette, her family's residence once served as a tavern along the Boston Post Road, situated alongside their property. This historic thoroughfare saw the passage of General Washington himself as he journeyed to and from Boston, undoubtedly on significant missions that shaped the course of American history.

Antonette's recollection vividly portrays the excitement and awe experienced by her father, John Bliss, and other young boys in the neighborhood. They eagerly gathered at the corner of the road, anticipating the sight of the esteemed general as he passed by. Their anticipation was met with immense gratification when General Washington, the "stately Chieftain," bestowed on them a gesture of acknowledgment—a bow—as he rode past.

Today, as we reflect on the pioneering postal route and stage line that once traversed Wilbraham, we honor the trailblazers who paved the way for progress and prosperity in our nation's history. Their story serves as a reminder of the transformative potential of visionary ideas and collaborative endeavors, inspiring us to continue pushing the boundaries of innovation and connectivity in the pursuit of a brighter future.

GENERAL KNOX'S EPIC EXPEDITION WITH HIS NOBLE TRAIN OF ARTILLERY THROUGH WILBRAHAM

Henry Knox was indeed a significant figure in early American history. Born in Boston in 1750, he played crucial roles in both the Revolutionary War and the early years of the U.S. government.

Knox began his career as a bookseller in Boston but soon became involved in the Patriot cause. During the onset of the American Revolutionary War following the Battles of Lexington and Concord in April 1775, Henry Knox, alongside his wife, Lucy, clandestinely departed Boston. Knox promptly joined the militia army while British troops were taking over the city. Utilizing his expertise in engineering, he played a pivotal role in fortifying the area under the command of General Artemas Ward.

As the conflict escalated, Knox found himself actively engaged in battle, notably directing rebel cannon fire during the pivotal Battle of Bunker Hill. His strategic acumen and dedication to the cause did not go unnoticed. When General George Washington assumed command of the Continental army in July 1775, he was deeply impressed by Knox's contributions.

A strong rapport swiftly developed between Washington and Knox, leading to regular interactions and collaboration with other high-ranking officers. Despite lacking a formal commission in the army initially, Knox's merit and potential were championed by figures such as John Adams in the Second Continental Congress.

Through concerted efforts, including Knox's own advocacy and strategic correspondence, he eventually secured a commission as colonel of the

Henry Knox, by Charles Wilson Peale. *National Portrait Gallery.*

army's artillery regiment. This achievement underscored Knox's growing stature within the Revolutionary ranks and his indispensable role in shaping the nascent Continental army's artillery strategy.

As the siege persisted, a pivotal idea emerged: the possibility of utilizing recently captured cannons from forts Ticonderoga and Crown Point in upstate New York to significantly influence its outcome. It is widely argued that Henry Knox proposed this notion to General Washington, who promptly entrusted him with the task of leading an expedition to retrieve the artillery.

Embarking on this critical mission, Knox arrived at Ticonderoga on December 5. Thus began what would later be dubbed the "noble train of artillery." Knox and his men commenced the arduous journey of transporting about sixty tons of cannons and other armaments. This herculean feat involved hauling the weaponry via horse-drawn and ox-drawn sleds across some three hundred miles of ice-covered rivers and snow-clad Berkshire Mountains to reach the besieged camps in Boston.

Knox's remarkable leadership and logistical prowess during this endeavor proved instrumental in bolstering the Continental army's artillery capabilities, ultimately playing a crucial role in the outcome of the siege. This daring exploit solidified Knox's reputation as an indispensable asset to the Revolutionary cause and further cemented his close relationship with General Washington.

In the sparsely populated region, Henry Knox faced significant challenges in recruiting personnel and securing draft animals for his expedition. Despite these obstacles, Knox and his team persevered, overcoming numerous difficulties along the way.

Henry Knox's journey with the cannons for General Washington traced a route that roughly followed the Old Boston Post Road through North Wilbraham on January 15 or January 16, 1776. This post road at that time would have come out of the town of Springfield along the north side of the present railroad tracks, meeting up to Stony Hill at the curve and following this road east onto the Old Boston Road and then going straight beyond the current bridge over the present railroad tracks and connecting to Boston Road. Following this road, it would have continued to Old Bay Road by Nine Mile Pond and back onto Boston Road. The road would then follow Maple Street to Mountain Road, continuing to the curve located at 138 where the road veered off in a northerly direction back onto Boston Road just after crossing the stone bridge over Spear Brook. Then continuing on Boston Road and crossing the heavy timber bridge over Twelve Mile Brook and on to the town of Palmer.

The historic pathway posed numerous challenges, especially navigating the muddy and snowy terrain, which pushed the limits of transportation by horse and oxen. One particularly challenging section was the steep grade from Mountain Road to Boston Road. Even General George Washington, on his way to Boston in 1775 to assume command of the Continental army, remarked in his diary about the difficulty of this part of the road.

Despite these formidable obstacles, Henry Knox demonstrated unwavering determination and resilience, pressing forward with his mission. His leadership and perseverance were instrumental in overcoming the challenges posed by the treacherous terrain, ensuring the successful transport of the cannons to General Washington's forces.

What was initially anticipated to be a two-week endeavor stretched into over six weeks of relentless effort. Finally, on January 27, 1776, Knox triumphantly reported the arrival of the weapons train to General Washington.

Knox's remarkable achievement is commemorated by a series of plaques marking the Henry Knox Trail in New York and Massachusetts, celebrating his pivotal role in the Revolutionary War. Among these commemorations, one notable plaque stands at the corner of Maple and Main Streets in Wilbraham.

Upon the arrival of the cannons in Cambridge, they were swiftly deployed to fortify Dorchester Heights, a strategic position recently seized by Washington's forces. The commanding presence of the new battery overlooking Boston Harbor compelled the British fleet to withdraw to Halifax, effectively ending the siege.

With this pivotal victory secured, Knox redirected his efforts toward strengthening defenses in Connecticut, Rhode Island and New York City, anticipating potential British assaults. During this time, he forged friendships with notable figures such as Alexander Hamilton, commander of the local artillery in New York, and Massachusetts General Benjamin Lincoln.

The location of the very first armory was approved by George Washington during the Revolutionary War. Henry Knox's familiarity with the area and its strategic significance played a crucial role in the selection of Springfield, Massachusetts, as the location for this armory. As Washington's artillery chief, Knox had an intimate knowledge of military logistics and strategic considerations. Before the recommendation of General Knox, Congress had already voted Brookfield, Massachusetts as the ideal site, but this was changed.

At the time of its establishment in 1777, Springfield was a small town. However, it possessed significant geographical advantages. Situated at the intersection of three rivers, including the important Connecticut River, and four major roads leading to key cities such as New York City, Boston, Albany and Montreal, Canada, Springfield was strategically located for transportation and defense purposes.

Moreover, Springfield's location just north of the Connecticut River's first waterfall, known as Enfield Falls, made it inaccessible to seafaring naval vessels. This natural barrier was protected from potential attacks by enemy ships, making Springfield the first town on the Connecticut River that was shielded from such threats.

The town of Wilbraham boasts a rich and storied history, with deep ties not only to local and regional narratives but also to significant chapters in national history, from its early settlement to its role in pivotal events like the American Revolutionary War.

Moreover, Wilbraham's connections to national history are exemplified by individuals like President George Washington and Henry Knox, whose remarkable expedition with the Noble Train of Artillery traversed the town's terrain en route to Boston during the Revolutionary War. This historic journey, commemorated by plaques along the Henry Knox Trail, highlights Wilbraham's integral role in the struggle for American independence and its enduring contributions to the nation's collective memory.

Beyond its Revolutionary War ties, Wilbraham's history encompasses diverse facets, including its agricultural heritage, industrial development and cultural evolution. From the iconic landmarks of yesteryear to the vibrant community institutions of today, Wilbraham's historic character continues to resonate with residents and visitors alike, offering a compelling narrative of resilience, progress and legacy.

TIMELESS CROSSING

THE STONE BRIDGE OF WILBRAHAM

Every day, numerous travelers pass along Boston Road in the vicinity of 2957 Boston Road, oblivious to the presence of a profoundly historic structure hidden beneath the driveway of a local business. This structure, a stone bridge dating back to 1732, stands as a silent witness to the tumultuous events of the American Revolution.

In 1732, alterations were made to the County Road, diverting it from its original course along the Bay Path, which had traversed this area since the late 1630s. Eastward of the Spear Brook hilltop, known today as Mountain Road, the old route was abandoned in favor of a new, more northeasterly path. This new section of road descended downhill briefly before intersecting with what is now Boston Road in the town.

The terrain of this newly constructed stretch posed significant challenges to travelers. Its steep gradient and rocky surface made it particularly treacherous. Notably, General George Washington himself remarked on these poor conditions during his journey along this road on June 30, 1775. This was a pivotal moment, as he was en route to Cambridge to assume command of the Continental army. Washington's scrutiny of the road's condition underscores its significance in the early stages of the Revolutionary War.

Subsequently, on October 22, 1789, Washington traversed this road once more, this time as the first president of the United States. His diary entry from this occasion vividly describes the rough and rocky nature of the terrain. Washington's journey along this route culminated in his resting approximately 1.9 miles east of the Wilbraham-Palmer town line. A memorial tablet now stands at this spot in Palmer, commemorating his brief respite and marking a poignant moment in American history.

In the summer of 1753, Benjamin Franklin undertook a pivotal expedition across this bridge, embarking on a mission to address the concerns of his Yankee clientele regarding postage fees. His meticulous survey of postal routes, including the original Upper Post Road passing through what is now Wilbraham, aimed to dispel doubts about the fairness of postal charges assessed by distance.

Nearly two decades later, in January 1776, Henry Knox traversed this bridge as he embarked on a daring mission to transport crucial artillery for General Washington's forces on the besieged Boston. Knox's legendary "Noble Train of Artillery" journeyed some three hundred miles, overcoming formidable obstacles of ice-covered rivers, snow-packed roads and some places muddy terrain to deliver essential weaponry to the Continental army.

The bridge also bore witness to the passage of British forces, including General Burgoyne's and his army in late October 1777 en route to Cambridge after surrendering his entire army in Saratoga New York, numbering 5,800. This was the greatest victory the American forces had up to that point in the Revolutionary War, and it proved to be the turning point in the war, as France entered into an alliance with the Americans. As prisoners of war, on November 7, 1778, the British soldiers were escorted to Charlottesville, Virginia. This time, General Burgoyne did not accompany his army, as he had been returned to the British at Newport, Rhode Island. About 4,145 troops and a number of baggage wagons made this journey, including General Riedesel, the commander of the German troops attached to Burgoyne, along with his wife and four young children. As they traversed the stone bridge, the British forces were diverted from their previous route east toward Cambridge. Instead, they turned south onto the West Road (Main Street) in Wilbraham, bypassing the main road to Springfield. This diversion was a strategic decision by the American forces, aiming to prevent the British from nearing the arsenal in Springfield once again. The British troops then encamped for the night in Wilbraham, likely near the town center, before continuing their journey toward Enfield, Connecticut. From there, they crossed the Connecticut River into Suffield and beyond as they pressed onward to Virginia.

The year 1787 marked a tumultuous chapter in Wilbraham's history, as Daniel Shays and his followers traversed this bridge during their infamous rebellion against economic injustices. The ensuing clash with Bowdoin's

The Old Stone Bridge as seen today. *David F. Bourcier.*

militia near the federal armory in Springfield would be remembered as Shays's Rebellion, a defining moment in the struggle for economic equality in post-revolutionary America.

Tragically, the area surrounding the bridge also witnessed darker events, notably the murder of Marcus Lyon in November 1805. Lyon's tragic end, with his body discovered near the bridge and his hat later uncovered beneath its arches, underscores the somber history of this area. Furthermore, the wrongful conviction and subsequent execution of Dominic Daly and James Halligan in 1806 cast a haunting shadow over the bridge, serving as a poignant reminder of the injustices perpetrated within its vicinity throughout history.

As the centuries have passed, the stone bridge near Boston Road remains an enduring symbol of the countless journeys, both heroic and tragic, that have shaped the course of American history. Its silent stones bear witness to the triumphs and tribulations of generations past, ensuring that their stories are not forgotten amid the passage of time.

During the 1976 Wilbraham Revolutionary Bicentennial celebration, the significance of the stone bridge near Boston Road was commemorated through various souvenirs adorned with artwork created by four esteemed local artists: William H. Gale, Wadsworth C. Hine, Paul Scopp and Richard C. Stevens. Their collective masterpiece depicted the iconic scene of General Henry Knox leading his team in hauling cannons from Ticonderoga across the ancient stone bridge spanning Spear Brook.

This artwork not only celebrated the historic journey of General Knox but also immortalized the enduring legacy of the stone bridge itself, which has stood firm against the ravages of time and weather, including floods. Despite the passage of centuries, this venerable structure continues to serve its purpose, linking the present with the past.

As a symbol of resilience and continuity, the old stone bridge remains an integral part of Wilbraham's heritage, a tangible reminder of the sacrifices and triumphs that have shaped the community's identity. Its presence is a testament to the enduring spirit of those who came before, inspiring reverence and admiration for generations to come.

A TALE OF CRAFTSMANSHIP AND COMMUNITY IN COLONIAL NEW ENGLAND

The Merrick tankard/chalice, meticulously crafted by the skilled hands of J. Potwine, stands as a testament to the artisan's legacy in the Boston area. Born in 1699 in England, Potwine journeyed to the New World, settling in Boston around 1700. His craftsmanship soon earned him renown, and by about 1715, he had become an esteemed member of the Congregational Church, his dedication to his craft matched only by his devotion to his faith.

In 1739, Potwine made the significant decision to relocate to Windsor, Connecticut, where he continued to ply his trade. However, tragedy struck, possibly due to the noxious fumes emitted during the smithing process, which may have ultimately cost him his sight. Despite this hardship, Potwine persevered, residing in East Windsor alongside his son until his passing around 1793.

Merrick tankard/chalice. *Atheneum Society of Wilbraham.*

The tankard/chalice, a masterpiece of Potwine's artistry, likely served as a poignant gift during a momentous occasion—perhaps as a wedding or ordination present, or even both. Its significance is deeply intertwined with the life and journey of Reverend Noah Merrick, a pivotal figure in the history of the Outward Commons, now known as Wilbraham and Hampden.

Reverend Noah Merrick, born on August 6, 1711, in West Springfield, rose to prominence within the community, ultimately finding his calling as a clergyman. His ordination, a pivotal event in the community's history, took place in June 1741 in Nathaniel Warriner's barn, amid the backdrop of a tempestuous sky that forced the congregation to seek shelter from the storm.

The tankard/chalice, bearing witness to the solemnity of Reverend Merrick's ordination, serves as a tangible link to this historical moment, embodying the spirit of resilience and perseverance that defined both Potwine and Merrick. Today, this cherished artifact finds its home in the museum at the Old Meeting House of Wilbraham alongside other relics that intertwine with the richness of Wilbraham's history and heritage. As visitors gaze at this tankard/chalice, they are invited to reflect on the enduring legacies of those who shaped the course of history in this corner of New England.

WILBRAHAM'S CONNECTION

THE ORDEAL OF BURGOYNE'S ARMY IN REVOLUTIONARY AMERICA

At the start of the American Revolution, the British recognized the strategic significance of controlling the water route connecting Lake Champlain, Lake George and the Hudson River. They believed that gaining control of this route would sever communication and supply lines between the northern and southern colonies, weakening the rebellion. Trouble had primarily brewed in New England, so the British aimed to quell the rebellion there, expecting the rest of the colonies to follow suit. In 1776, the British, led by General William Howe, successfully captured New York City and parts of the lower Hudson Valley.

However, their advance from Canada, led by General Guy Carleton, was halted at Fort Ticonderoga, and they were forced to retreat due to harsh winter conditions. In 1777, General John Burgoyne, who had been part of the failed Canadian expedition, proposed a renewed effort to seize control of the waterway. His plan, outlined in "Thoughts for Conducting the War on the Side of Canada," aimed to strengthen the existing strategy in New York, and it gained approval from Lord Germain. Burgoyne was appointed to lead the new campaign, marking a significant moment in the British strategy during the American Revolution.

The Campaign of 1777 was a pivotal moment in the American Revolution, marked by a coordinated effort by British forces to gain control of strategic points in the colonies. General John Burgoyne was tasked with advancing south from Canada through Lake Champlain, capturing Fort Ticonderoga and proceeding along the Hudson River to Albany. Meanwhile, General Sir William Howe was to advance north from New York City to Albany, where the two forces would converge. Additionally, Barry St. Leger was to lead a third force west along the Mohawk River Valley, serving as a diversion and securing a western water route between Canada and New York City by recruiting Loyalists.

However, the plan faced significant challenges. Howe became preoccupied with a campaign to capture Philadelphia, delaying his advance to Albany. St. Leger's force became embroiled in a prolonged siege of Fort Stanwix and was eventually forced to retreat to Canada as American forces closed in. Despite these setbacks, Burgoyne remained unaware of his colleagues' difficulties and continued his march toward Albany.

The disjointed nature of the British strategy, coupled with unforeseen obstacles, ultimately contributed to the failure of the Campaign of 1777 and had significant ramifications for the course of the American Revolution.

After capturing Ticonderoga with ease and speed that shook Patriot morale, Burgoyne continued his march south, defeating American troops at Hubbardton and forcing the evacuation of Forts Anne and Edward. Then his luck began to run out. A column of Hessians (German mercenaries) he sent to raid Bennington was defeated by troops under Brigadier General John Stark and Lieutenant Colonel Seth Warner. Continuing southward, Burgoyne crossed near present-day Stillwater, where the Americans under Horatio Gates, who had replaced Philip Schuyler as American commander, had taken up position on Bemis Heights. Burgoyne tried to break through the American lines at Freeman's Farm (September 19) and at Bemis Heights (October 7). Both attempts failed, and the British commander, finding himself outnumbered and surrounded and unable to retreat, surrendered on October 17, 1777.

Burgoyne's defeat and surrender at Saratoga, coupled with the victory months prior at Fort Stanwix, led directly to the alliances between the United States, France and the Netherlands. These alliances helped to sustain the new United States throughout the rest of the war and directly contributed to the final victory and British surrender at Yorktown in 1781.

Following the Battle of Saratoga, instead of demanding Burgoyne's surrender, General Gates offered to enter into a convention with him. This convention, known as the Convention of Saratoga, was a formal treaty that temporarily halted hostilities between the two armies. Under its terms, Burgoyne and his soldiers were allowed to return to England on the condition that they would not take up arms against America again.

Per the terms of surrender, the British on October 17 marched out with honors, grounded their arms and began a two-hundred-mile trek to Boston. In late October, General Burgoyne and his army numbering about 5,800 soldiers marched through the town of Wilbraham on the Post Road and crossed the stone bridge over Spear Brook that can still be seen today.

However, this generous treatment of Burgoyne and his army sparked outrage among Revolutionary Americans. Throughout the conflict, British forces treated American prisoners harshly, leading to overcrowded prisons and appalling conditions on disease-ridden prison ships. In response to public outcry, the Continental Congress suspended the Convention of Saratoga, deciding to keep Burgoyne's army in American captivity for the remainder of the war, which lasted more than five and a half years.

Yet Congress faced a dilemma, as it lacked the resources to support the British prisoners. With the British unwilling to reimburse Congress for their expenses and Congress struggling to even provide for its troops, a dire situation arose. In desperation, Congress devised a solution that would have unforeseen and disastrous consequences for the British captives.

Following the suspension of the Convention of Saratoga, Congress took immediate action to address the situation of the British prisoners. Originally slated to be transported from Boston back to England, the prisoners faced resistance from the local population, who vehemently opposed hosting the costly and disgruntled redcoats. With Massachusetts refusing to provide for them, Congress decided to relocate the prisoners to Charlottesville, Virginia. Now prisoners of war, Burgoyne's army was marched south, though without their general, who had been returned to the British in Newport, Rhode Island. On November 7, 1778, approximately 4,145 troops, along with numerous baggage wagons, undertook this journey. Among them was General Riedesel, commander of the German troops allied with Burgoyne. As the column traversed the Post Road and the stone bridge in Wilbraham, the British forces were diverted from their previous route east toward Boston. Instead, they turned south onto the West Road (now Main Street) in Wilbraham, bypassing the main route to Springfield. This strategic diversion by the American forces aimed to keep the British away from the Springfield arsenal. That night, the British troops encamped in Wilbraham, likely near the town center, before continuing south toward Enfield, Connecticut. From Enfield, they crossed the Connecticut River into Suffield and pressed onward to Virginia.

The journey to Charlottesville was arduous, spanning hundreds of miles and taking place during a harsh winter. Upon arrival, the prisoners were

Painting of John Burgoyne's surrender to Horatio Gates on October 17, 1777. *National Archives and Records Administration.*

greeted with dire conditions: scarce food and no shelter. The local populace regarded them with a mixture of hostility and opportunism. Merchants and farmers sought to profit from their presence by selling goods at exorbitant prices, while militia guards often mistreated the defenseless captives, venting their frustrations on them.

The relocation of the British prisoners to Virginia only exacerbated their suffering, subjecting them to exploitation and abuse at the hands of both civilians and militia personnel.

BIBLIOGRAPHY

Celularo Paris. *Joan D. Wilbraham History and Culture*. Vol. 4, *1963–2013*. Tell Tale Books Publishing, 2015.

Chase, Levi Badger. *The Bay Path and Along the Way*. Original print. Leopold Classic Library, 1919.

Clark, Jim Adams. Cemetery Walking Tour. Student Activities, Department of MRHS, 2007.

Dexter, Lincoln A. *Wilbraham*. U.S.A. Bicentennial Committee Concerning Wilbraham and the American Revolution, 1975.

The First Church of Wilbraham. *Historical Sketch of the First Church of Wilbraham*. 1916.

Gray, Coralie M. *Wilbraham*. Images of America series. Arcadia Publishing, 2001.

Holland, Josiah G. *History of Western Massachusetts*. Vol. 2, Part 3. Samuel Bowles and Company, 1855.

Howlett, Carl C. *Early Hampden Its Settlers and the Homes They Built*. Yola Guild of the Federated Community Church, 1958.

Massachusetts Historical Commission. *Historic & Archaeological Resources of the Connecticut River Valley*. 2007.

Merrick, Charles L. *History of Wilbraham*. U.S.A. Bicentennial ed., 1763–1963. Polygraphic Company of America Inc., 1964.

Noon, Alfred A.M. *The History of Ludlow*. Springfield Printing and Binding Company, 1912.

Peck, Chauncey E. *The History of Wilbraham*. Reprint, Higginson Book Company. Originally printed in 1913.

———. *Minneola and the Parson's Rose Poems*. Press of Carpenter & Morehouse, 1904.

Stebbins, Rufus P. *Historical Address, Centennial Celebration, Town of Wilbraham*. George C. Rand & Avery Printers, 1864.

Tingle, Bruce J. *Military Rolls of the Outward Commons, Soldiers of Wilbraham*. Heritage Books, 2000.

Warriner, Edwin, Reverend. *The Warriner Family History of New England Origin*. Joel Munsell's Sons, Publisher, 1899.

Watters, David Markers, III. *The Journal of the Association for Gravestones Studies*. University Press of America Inc., 1985.

Williams, Melvin G. *The Last Words*. Oldstone Enterprises, 1973.

Newspapers

Boston Transcript.
Springfield Daily News.
Springfield Republican.
Springfield Union.
Wilbraham and Hampden Times.

Websites

abc.net.au/news.
americanhistorycentral.com.
archive.nytimes.com/wheels.blogs.nytimes.com.
bostonpostcane.org/the-canes.
britannica.com.
historicengland.org.uk.
historic-northampton.org/daleyandhalligan/dh_resources.html.
history.com.
mericashistoryllc.com.
newenglandhistoricalsociety.com.
nps.gov/index.htm.
nps.gov/spar/learn/historyculture/federal-armories.htm.
publicdomainreview.org.
springfieldmuseums.org/about/museum-of-springfield-history/springfield-history-library-archive.

ushistory.org/valleyforge//index.html.
wikipedia.org/wiki/Main_Page.
wikisource.org/wiki/Main_Page.
worldhistory.org.

Institutions

Atheneum Society of Wilbraham, Old Meeting House Museum. Historical archives.
Hampden Historical Society. Historical archives.
Hampden Town Library. Historical archives.
Springfield Armory National Historic Site.
Springfield Museums.
Wilbraham Town Library. Historical archives.

ABOUT THE AUTHOR

David F. Bourcier and Marty.
David F. Bourcier.

David Bourcier is a retired fire chief and a local historian from Wilbraham, Massachusetts, who has a deep passion for the history of his town. With a keen eye for detail and a love of storytelling, Bourcier has become known for his engaging and informative short stories about the people and events that have shaped Wilbraham over the years. From the town's early days as a colonial settlement to its growth and development in the twentieth century, Bourcier's writing brings the history of Wilbraham to life in a way that is both educational and entertaining. Bourcier's website, Wilbraham Historical Tidbits, explores some of the fascinating stories he has uncovered in his research. Whether you're a longtime resident of Wilbraham or simply interested in the history of small New England towns, you won't want to miss this glimpse into the world of local history. Bourcier is also the president of the Atheneum Society of Wilbraham, which maintains the Old Meeting House and Hearse House Museums located at 450 Main Street, Wilbraham. In addition to this, Bourcier is a cemetery commissioner who is responsible for Adams Cemetery. This cemetery is the oldest in town and dates back to 1736.

Visit us at
www.historypress.com